Gallbladder Wellness:

Gallbladder Pain, Gallstones, Biliary Colic Attacks, Cholecystitis and Cholecystectomy Recovery Guide

Table of Contents

INTRODUCTION

Navigating the complexities of gallbladder health extends beyond those who've undergone removal surgery; it's equally pertinent for individuals striving to preserve their gallbladder, aiming to alleviate pain, dissolve stones, and restore full functionality. As the author of this comprehensive guide, I've traversed the terrain of gallbladder health, dedicating over a year to understanding the spectrum of challenges faced by those striving to retain their gallbladder's health and those seeking guidance after surgical removal.

My personal quest for well-being sparked a deep dive into gallbladder health, spurred by firsthand experiences wrestling with discomfort, stone formation, and the uncertainties of surgical intervention. This book is an outcome of my quest for answers, amalgamating personal insights, medical expertise, and a fervent desire to extend a helping hand to individuals facing similar tribulations.

"Gallbladder Wellness: Tips, Recipes, and Post-Removal Diet Guide" isn't solely tailored for post-removal individuals; it's a comprehensive guide encompassing strategies for pain management, dietary considerations, and lifestyle adjustments for all stages of gallbladder health. Whether one seeks to preserve their gallbladder, dissolve stones, regain functionality, or adjust to life post-surgery, the recipes and guidance within these pages serve as a compass.

Through meticulous research and consultations, this guide articulates the significance of diet, stress management, and holistic approaches for gallbladder well-being. It doesn't just offer recipes; it presents a spectrum of solutions—practical, dietary, and emotional—for those embarking on a journey toward gallbladder health and those embracing life after its removal.

This book stands as a beacon of hope for anyone seeking relief, empowerment, and a renewed perspective on gallbladder health. It's my fervent aspiration that this guide becomes a companion, offering solace, empowerment, and a roadmap toward living well despite the challenges of gallbladder-related concerns.

Anatomy and Function of the Gallbladder

The gallbladder, a seemingly unassuming organ tucked beneath the liver, plays a pivotal role in our digestive system. Often overlooked until trouble arises, this small, pear-shaped pouch acts as a reservoir for bile, the golden elixir crucial for fat digestion and absorption.

Picture this: nestled snugly against the underside of the liver, the gallbladder resembles a miniature pouch, about 7-10 centimeters in length when fully distended. Its primary function? To store and concentrate bile, that unsung hero produced by the liver cells, which journeys through intricate bile ducts to reach its destination.

Bile, often likened to a digestive detergent, is a concoction of bile salts, cholesterol, bilirubin, and other compounds essential for breaking down dietary fats. Here's where the gallbladder steps in, acting as a storage facility for this vital fluid. When we consume a meal, especially one rich in fats, the gallbladder contracts, releasing concentrated bile into the small intestine through the bile ducts.

This release of bile facilitates the emulsification of fats, breaking them down into smaller droplets that enzymes find easier to digest. Imagine the gallbladder as a strategic partner in the digestive orchestra, precisely timing the release of bile to ensure efficient fat breakdown, absorption of vital nutrients, and the body's energy supply.

However, this seemingly humble organ isn't without its woes. Gallstones, those crystalline formations composed of cholesterol or bilirubin, can form within the gallbladder, leading to discomfort, pain, and even inflammation. Such conditions can disrupt the gallbladder's function, impacting its ability to store and release bile effectively, and sometimes necessitating its removal.

Understanding the gallbladder's anatomy and function underscores the significance of its role in our digestive symphony. It serves as a reminder of the intricate mechanisms orchestrating our body's digestion, urging us to nurture and care for this often-forgotten yet indispensable organ. From dietary choices to lifestyle habits, preserving gallbladder health becomes a cornerstone in fostering overall well-being and digestive harmony.

COMMON GALLBLADDER DISORDERS

One prevalent issue affecting the gallbladder is the formation of gallstones. These crystalline formations, often composed of cholesterol or bilirubin, can range in size from minuscule specks to substantial stones that impede the gallbladder's function. These stones may not elicit symptoms initially, but they can lead to excruciating pain if they obstruct the bile ducts, causing what is commonly known as a gallbladder «attack.» These attacks manifest as intense upper abdominal pain, often radiating to the back or shoulder, accompanied by nausea and vomiting.

Cholecystitis, another common disorder, involves inflammation of the gallbladder. This inflammation can be acute or chronic, with acute cases typically stemming from gallstones obstructing the cystic duct, leading to a buildup of bile and subsequent inflammation. Chronic cholecystitis may develop over time, marked by repeated bouts of inflammation that gradually impair the gallbladder's function.

Gallbladder polyps, though less common, are growths that can develop within the gallbladder wall. While most polyps are benign, some have the potential to become cancerous. Monitoring these polyps through imaging studies and, in some cases, surgical removal might be necessary to prevent complications.

Biliary dyskinesia, characterized by abnormal gallbladder contractions, can result in inefficient bile release, causing symptoms akin to those of gallstones or cholecystitis. Patients may experience abdominal pain and digestive disturbances without the presence of gallstones.

The diagnosis of gallbladder disorders often involves a combination of medical history assessment, physical examination, and imaging tests like ultrasound or CT scans. Treatment strategies vary depending on the specific disorder and its severity. Gallstones may be managed through medication to dissolve them, but surgical removal of the gallbladder, known as cholecystectomy, is a common and effective solution, often relieving symptoms and preventing recurrence.

Lifestyle modifications play a pivotal role in managing and preventing gallbladder disorders. A balanced diet, low in saturated fats and cholesterol, can reduce the risk of gallstone formation. Incorporating fiber-rich foods, staying hydrated, and avoiding rapid weight fluctuations contribute to overall gallbladder health.

In conclusion, understanding the spectrum of common gallbladder disorders empowers individuals to recognize symptoms, seek timely medical intervention, and adopt preventive measures. These insights underscore the importance of digestive health and highlight the significance of nurturing habits conducive to gallbladder well-being, ultimately fostering a harmonious relationship with this often-underestimated yet vital organ.

FORMATION OF GALLSTONES

The formation of gallstones, a fascinating yet potentially troublesome occurrence within the gallbladder, unveils a complex interplay of biological factors. These crystalline formations, often composed of cholesterol or bilirubin, represent a significant concern in digestive health, warranting a deeper exploration into their intricate genesis.

At the core of gallstone formation lies an imbalance in the constituents of bile, the golden elixir produced by the liver to aid in fat digestion. When this delicate equilibrium is disrupted, it sets the stage for the genesis of these crystalline structures. Cholesterol gallstones, the most prevalent type, typically stem from an excess of cholesterol in bile. This surplus cholesterol precipitates into solid crystals, gradually forming into stones within the gallbladder.

The cascade of events leading to cholesterol gallstone formation is multifaceted. It often begins with the supersaturation of bile with cholesterol, where the cholesterol concentration surpasses the fluid's capacity to dissolve it. Under such conditions, cholesterol starts to crystallize, forming microscopic particles known as microcrystals. These minute particles, akin to a seed, serve as the nucleus for gallstone development.

However, the journey from microcrystals to substantial gallstones isn't immediate. These nascent crystals require time and conditions conducive to their growth and aggregation. Factors such as stasis or reduced motility within the gallbladder, which impedes the complete emptying of bile, create an environment ripe for these microcrystals to conglomerate. Over time, these aggregations of cholesterol crystals merge and solidify, evolving into the palpable gallstones that can vary in size and composition.

Pigment gallstones, less common than their cholesterol counterparts, form through a different mechanism. These stones result from an excess of bilirubin, a breakdown product of red blood cells, which accumulates in bile. High levels of bilirubin can lead to the precipitation and aggregation of bilirubin molecules, resulting in the formation of pigment stones.

The journey through gallstone formation can be silent, with these crystalline structures residing within the gallbladder without causing noticeable symptoms. However, when these stones obstruct the flow of bile or trigger spasms within the gallbladder, they can elicit a range of uncomfortable sensations, including acute and intense pain in the abdomen, often radiating to the back or shoulder.

In essence, the genesis of gallstones is a complex amalgamation of cholesterol or bilirubin imbalance, supersaturation of bile, and conducive conditions within the gallbladder.

Understanding this intricate process underscores the importance of maintaining bile equilibrium and adopting habits conducive to gallbladder health. This comprehension serves as a cornerstone in proactive management, ultimately fostering digestive harmony and well-being.

SYMPTOMS OF GALLSTONES FORMATION: UNDERSTANDING THE PRELUDE TO DISCOMFORT

The formation of gallstones within the gallbladder, while often asymptomatic in its early stages, can gradually manifest into a range of discomforting sensations and symptoms. Delving into the nuanced landscape of these symptoms provides a crucial insight into the evolving narrative of gallstone formation and its impact on an individual's well-being.

At the inception of gallstone formation, individuals might not experience any overt symptoms. These crystalline formations can exist silently within the gallbladder, gradually developing without causing noticeable discomfort. However, as these stones grow in size or migrate within the gallbladder, they can provoke a cascade of sensations, signaling the body's response to their presence.

One of the hallmark symptoms attributed to gallstone formation is biliary colic—an abrupt onset of intense, gripping pain in the upper abdomen or right shoulder. This pain, often described as excruciating and intermittent, can persist for hours and typically occurs after consuming fatty or heavy meals. The severity of this pain can disrupt daily activities, leading individuals to seek immediate medical attention.

Accompanying this intense pain, individuals might experience nausea and vomiting. These symptoms often arise as a consequence of the gallstones obstructing the bile ducts or triggering spasms within the gallbladder. The distress caused by these symptoms can significantly impact an individual's quality of life, leading to discomfort, anxiety, and a decreased appetite.

In some cases, particularly when gallstones cause inflammation of the gallbladder (cholecystitis), additional symptoms might emerge. These can include fever, persistent abdominal pain that doesn't subside, and tenderness in the abdomen upon touch, signaling a more acute phase in the progression of gallstone-related complications.

Notably, while some individuals might experience pronounced symptoms indicative of gallstone formation, others may remain asymptomatic, unaware of the presence of these crystalline entities until detected incidentally during routine medical examinations or imaging studies.

Accurate diagnosis of gallstones and their associated symptoms often involves a comprehensive evaluation by healthcare professionals. Imaging techniques like ultrasound, CT scans, or MRIs play a pivotal role in visualizing gallstones within the gallbladder and determining their size, quantity, and potential impact on an individual's health.

In essence, understanding the nuanced symptoms associated with gallstone formation is pivotal in recognizing potential issues and seeking timely medical intervention. These symptoms, often characterized by intense abdominal pain, nausea, and vomiting, serve as red flags prompting individuals to navigate towards proactive management and preventive measures conducive to gallbladder health.

CHOLECYSTITIS: INFLAMMATION OF THE GALLBLADDER

Cholecystitis, an inflammation of the gallbladder, presents a tumultuous chapter in the narrative of digestive health. This condition, often arising from gallstones obstructing the cystic duct, marks a significant departure from the silent existence of these crystalline formations, catapulting individuals into a realm of discomfort and potential complications.

At its core, cholecystitis is a consequence of obstructed bile flow within the gallbladder. Gallstones, those crystalline entities formed from cholesterol or bilirubin, can hinder the proper drainage of bile, leading to a buildup of this digestive fluid within the gallbladder. This stagnant bile serves as a breeding ground for inflammation, initiating a cascade of events that result in gallbladder irritation, swelling, and pain.

The hallmark of cholecystitis is persistent and intense abdominal pain, typically localized in the upper right quadrant. This pain, distinct from the intermittent biliary colic associated with gallstone formation, often lingers for hours or days, becoming more relentless and debilitating. It might radiate to the right shoulder or back and intensify after consuming fatty or greasy foods. Accompanying this pain, individuals might experience tenderness in the abdomen upon touch, further exacerbating their discomfort.

As cholecystitis progresses, additional symptoms may manifest, signaling a more acute phase of gallbladder inflammation. Fever, chills, and an elevated white blood cell count might indicate the body's heightened immune response to the inflamed gallbladder, suggesting a potential infection complicating the condition.

Diagnosing cholecystitis involves a thorough medical evaluation, including a review of symptoms, physical examination, and imaging studies. Ultrasound imaging remains a primary diagnostic tool, allowing visualization of gallbladder inflammation, thickened gallbladder walls, and the presence of gallstones or related complications.

Management of cholecystitis often necessitates medical intervention, especially in severe or recurrent cases. In acute cholecystitis, treatment might involve fasting to rest the gallbladder, intravenous fluids for hydration, and antibiotics to address any associated infection. Surgical removal of the gallbladder, known as cholecystectomy, is often considered the definitive solution, offering relief from recurrent inflammation and preventing future complications.

Prevention of cholecystitis revolves around mitigating gallstone formation and adopting lifestyle changes conducive to gallbladder health. This includes maintaining a balanced diet, avoiding rapid weight fluctuations, and steering clear of excessive consumption of high-fat or greasy foods.

In essence, understanding cholecystitis and its associated symptoms is pivotal in navigating potential complications arising from gallstone-related inflammation. This comprehension underscores the importance of timely medical intervention, proactive management, and preventive measures aimed at preserving gallbladder health and fostering digestive harmony.

The Role of Visceral Massage in Alleviating Gallbladder Pain

Gallbladder attacks are notorious for their excruciating pain and discomfort, often prompting a quest for immediate relief. In this pursuit, visceral massage emerges as a promising therapeutic intervention, offering potential comfort and relief during these distressing episodes.

Visceral massage, a specialized technique targeting internal organs, aims to release tension, enhance circulation, and restore optimal function within the body. Specifically tailored for the abdomen, this technique involves gentle, rhythmic manipulation designed to alleviate tension and induce relaxation.

During a gallbladder attack, the intensity of pain stemming from gallstones or inflammation can be overwhelming. Visceral massage, skillfully administered by a trained practitioner, focuses on the affected abdominal area. By applying gentle pressure and specific massage techniques, it seeks to reduce tension, potentially providing relief amidst the acute discomfort of an attack.

The mechanics of visceral massage are rooted in its ability to stimulate the parasympathetic nervous system, promoting a state of relaxation. This relaxation response can potentially alleviate spasms, ease constriction within bile ducts, and offer respite from the sharp, stabbing pain characteristic of gallbladder attacks.

Beyond immediate pain relief, regular sessions of visceral massage may contribute to overall gallbladder health. By improving circulation, reducing tension in the abdominal region, and optimizing organ function, it may play a role in preventing or reducing the frequency of gallbladder-related issues.

However, it's important to regard visceral massage as a supplementary, rather than sole, therapeutic approach for gallbladder problems. When integrated with conventional medical treatments, it can offer additional support and relief. Consulting healthcare professionals is paramount before considering visceral massage, especially in cases of acute or severe symptoms. Their assessment ensures the massage is safe, appropriate, and beneficial for individual circumstances.

In conclusion, visceral massage stands as a non-invasive and potentially effective method for managing the intense pain accompanying gallbladder attacks. Its emphasis on inducing relaxation and reducing tension within the abdominal area presents a complementary approach to conventional treatments. When administered by a qualified professional and in conjunction with medical advice, visceral massage holds promise as a tool to mitigate the severity of gallbladder-related pain and discomfort.

Gallbladder Stones: A Time Bomb with Uncertain Outcomes

The presence of gallbladder stones is akin to a ticking time bomb, the detonation of which remains unpredictable, carrying unforeseen consequences for an individual's health and well-being. The uncertainty surrounding when and how these stones might cause distress looms ominously.

Gallbladder stones, often silent in their formation, can escalate into severe complications at any moment. The intermittent nature of symptoms, ranging from mild discomfort to excruciating pain, renders the situation precarious. The unpredictability of a stone's movement within the bile ducts brings forth the looming threat of acute episodes, leading to severe pain, jaundice, or even pancreatitis.

Furthermore, an untreated gallbladder with stones can adversely affect the functioning of other vital organs, primarily the liver and pancreas. The gallbladder's role in storing and releasing bile, essential for fat digestion, can be disrupted. The imbalance in bile flow not only affects digestion but also exerts undue stress on the liver and pancreas. Over time, this stress may contribute to liver issues or pancreatitis, amplifying the complexities of the situation.

The intricate relationship between the gallbladder, liver, and pancreas underscores the interdependency of these organs in the digestive process. An ailing gallbladder not only jeopardizes its own functionality but also disrupts the harmonious coordination among these vital organs, potentially triggering a cascade of health issues.

Neglecting the removal of a gallbladder plagued by stones is akin to playing a hazardous waiting game. The risks associated with such a gamble extend beyond the occasional discomfort to the realm of severe complications and long-term organ dysfunction. Consequently, the decision to delay intervention can exacerbate the situation, posing a significant threat to an individual's health and overall well-being.

In conclusion, the presence of gallbladder stones should not be taken lightly. It's imperative to recognize their potential to wreak havoc on the body, not only through acute episodes but also through long-term repercussions on essential organs. Timely intervention and the removal of the gallbladder, when necessary, stand as critical measures to prevent the ticking time bomb of gallstones from causing irreparable harm.

PRESERVING OR REMOVING THE GALLBLADDER: A MATTER OF CONSIDERATION AND UNDERSTANDING

The decision to retain or remove the gallbladder hinges on specific circumstances and the patient's condition. However, there are situations where fear of surgery and misunderstanding of risks might lead to choosing to retain the gallbladder, which in some cases could heighten health risks.

Many individuals fear surgeries and opt to keep their gallbladder, even when it becomes problematic. They might consult doctors offering methods to dissolve stones, hoping to avoid surgery. However, this approach might be temporary and fails to address the underlying cause of stone formation. Moreover, even if stones are fragmented, they can recur, causing further episodes.

In cases of gallstone formation and ignoring symptoms, there's a risk of bile duct blockage. When stones move, they can cause severe pain, but attempting to maneuver them through the body can result in a risk of fatality. In such instances, surgery may become the sole means to prevent severe complications.

Furthermore, the gallbladder should not be retained if it's non-functional, doesn't contract, is completely obstructed by stones, and fails to perform its function.

Understanding the risks and potential complications of keeping a problematic gallbladder is crucial. Surgery, contrary to popular belief, is often minimally invasive, and individuals recover quickly, leading pain-free lives. The fear of surgery shouldn't outweigh the potential health hazards associated with retaining a dysfunctional gallbladder.

UNDERSTANDING GALLBLADDER ISSUES: A HOLISTIC VIEW FROM NEW GERMAN MEDICINE AND ESOTERIC INSIGHTS

In the realm of holistic healing, the connection between emotional well-being and physical health stands as a fundamental tenet. According to the principles of New German Medicine and esoteric perspectives, issues concerning the gallbladder often intertwine with an individual's emotional landscape and energy dynamics.

The core thesis posits that emotional states, particularly negative ones like anger and aggression, can significantly impact the health of the gallbladder. When a person navigates a lifestyle or circumstances where they feel compelled to defend their territory or personal space, these emotions can manifest and create disturbances within the gallbladder's functioning. It is believed that these emotions can lead to stagnation or uncontrolled releases of bile, ultimately contributing to the formation of gallstones and subsequent issues.

Living in a state of chronic stress, perpetually without relaxation or moments of mental calmness, also contributes to this scenario. Stress amplifies the negative emotional responses and exacerbates the potential for disruptions in the gallbladder's equilibrium.

The intricate connection between emotions and physical health, particularly regarding the gallbladder, underscores the importance of addressing emotional well-being in holistic treatment approaches. Techniques such as meditation and relaxation practices play a pivotal role in rebalancing emotional states and reducing stress. By fostering a sense of mental tranquility and releasing pent-up negative emotions, individuals can potentially alleviate the burden on the gallbladder and mitigate the risk of issues associated with bile stasis and stone formation.

In the context of gallbladder treatment, it's crucial to consider this holistic perspective. Beyond conventional medical interventions, integrating practices that promote emotional balance, stress reduction, and relaxation into the treatment regimen could offer comprehensive care and potentially prevent recurrence of gallbladder issues.

In conclusion, New German Medicine and esoteric viewpoints emphasize the intricate interplay between emotions, stress, and gallbladder health. Acknowledging and addressing emotional well-being, incorporating relaxation practices, and fostering mental equilibrium stand as vital components in holistic approaches to gallbladder health and healing. Integrating these holistic practices alongside conventional medical treatments could pave the way for a more comprehensive and effective approach to managing gallbladder issues.

MANAGING GALLBLADDER ISSUES NATURALLY

When it comes to treating gallbladder issues using herbs and natural remedies, it's crucial to realize that self-treatment without consulting a doctor can be both risky and inappropriate. If an individual chooses to use herbs or natural methods to eliminate gallstones, they should be under the supervision of a qualified medical professional.

Self-medication can lead to serious complications, especially concerning gallstones. Uncontrolled use of herbs or unprofessional therapy may cause the movement or blockage of gallstones, or even their fragmentation, leading to acute pain and severe complications.

It's important to note that even when using herbs or natural methods, regular monitoring of gallstone status through ultrasound examinations (ultrasounds) under a doctor's supervision is essential. This allows tracking the effectiveness of the chosen therapy and preventing potential complications associated with self-treatment.

Decisions regarding treating gallbladder issues with herbs or natural remedies should be made in consultation with a medical professional. They can evaluate the patient's condition, assess potential risks, and choose the most effective and safe treatment.

Diet and Nutrition for Gallbladder Health

The gallbladder, a small yet integral part of the digestive system, plays a crucial role in storing and concentrating bile—a fluid that aids in digesting fats. Problems related to bile flow and discomfort in the gallbladder often call for dietary adjustments aimed at easing symptoms and promoting better digestive health.

Understanding the Role of Diet in Gallbladder Health:

Diet plays a pivotal role in managing conditions associated with bile flow issues and gallbladder discomfort. Certain dietary choices can either alleviate or exacerbate symptoms, emphasizing the importance of a well-balanced and mindful eating regimen.

Foods to Avoid:

Fatty, greasy, and fried foods are commonly recognized as triggers for gallbladder discomfort. These foods stimulate the gallbladder to release bile, potentially causing pain or discomfort, especially in those prone to gallbladder issues. Additionally, highly processed foods, refined sugars, and excessive consumption of red meat may contribute to exacerbating symptoms.

Gallbladder-Friendly Foods:

In contrast, incorporating a diet rich in fiber, fresh fruits, vegetables, and lean proteins can support gallbladder health. Fiber aids in digestion and helps regulate cholesterol levels, potentially reducing the risk of gallstone formation. Foods high in omega-3 fatty acids, such as salmon or flaxseeds, may have anti-inflammatory properties, potentially benefiting individuals experiencing gallbladder discomfort.

Hydration and Moderation:

Staying adequately hydrated is crucial for maintaining gallbladder health. Drinking sufficient water throughout the day can aid in the digestion and flow of bile, potentially reducing the risk of gallstone formation. Moreover, portion control and moderation in meal sizes can prevent overwhelming the gallbladder with excessive amounts of food at once, reducing the chances of discomfort.

Meal Timing and Consistency:

Establishing regular meal times and avoiding prolonged fasting can help maintain consistent bile flow. Skipping meals or prolonged periods without eating might cause the gallbladder to contract less frequently, potentially leading to stagnant bile and discomfort.

Conclusion:

In essence, adopting a gallbladder-friendly diet involves making thoughtful food choices that support digestive health. Prioritizing whole foods, fiber-rich options, lean proteins, staying hydrated, and maintaining portion control can contribute significantly to managing symptoms related to bile flow issues and gallbladder discomfort. However, individual responses to dietary changes may vary, so consulting a healthcare professional or a registered dietitian is advisable for personalized guidance in managing gallbladder-related concerns through dietary modifications.

Starting Your Day Right: The Importance of a Balanced Breakfast

Beginning your day with a well-rounded breakfast sets the tone for your body's functions and energy levels. It's not about overindulgence or consuming high-fat meals but rather about incorporating essential elements like fats, omega-3s, and vegetables in moderate amounts.

The Balanced Breakfast Formula:

A balanced breakfast should ideally include a moderate amount of fats, particularly those containing omega-3 fatty acids, alongside vegetables. This isn't about excessive fats but rather a healthy dose sufficient for facilitating bile flow and kickstarting the digestive system.

Focusing on Healthy Fats and Omega-3s:

Incorporating sources of healthy fats and omega-3s, such as avocados, nuts, or seeds, in your breakfast can support gallbladder health and aid in digestion. These fats, in controlled portions, play a vital role in promoting bile flow without overwhelming the system.

The Role of Bitter and Acidic Foods:

Including bitter and acidic foods in your breakfast can also contribute to stimulating bile flow. Some types of greens, known for their bitter taste, and fermented or pickled vegetables with their acidic nature can trigger the release of bile, aiding in the digestive process.

A Balanced Approach:

It's crucial to strike a balance; the objective isn't to load up on excessive fats or heavy foods but to incorporate a variety of elements that support digestion and gallbladder health. Small amounts of the right fats, omega-3 sources, and a mix of vegetables, bitter greens, and acidic foods can initiate bile flow without causing discomfort.

Conclusion:

Starting your day with a breakfast that includes these elements in moderation sets the stage for a well-functioning digestive system. It's about providing your body with the right components to kickstart digestion and ensure gallbladder health, without overloading your system. This balanced approach to breakfast can promote optimal digestion and overall well-being throughout the day.

Lifestyle Changes to Support Gallbladder Function

Beyond dietary adjustments, lifestyle changes play a pivotal role in supporting gallbladder health and preventing potential discomfort or complications. Embracing certain habits and modifications in daily routines can significantly contribute to the well-being of this crucial digestive organ.

Hydration and Fluid Intake:

Maintaining adequate hydration is fundamental for gallbladder health. Drinking sufficient water throughout the day facilitates bile flow and aids in the digestion of fats, reducing the risk of gallstone formation.

Regular Physical Activity:

Incorporating regular exercise into daily routines is key. Engaging in moderate physical activities like walking, jogging, or yoga not only helps in maintaining a healthy weight but also supports overall digestive health, reducing the likelihood of gallbladder issues linked to a sedentary lifestyle.

Stress Management and Relaxation Techniques:

Chronic stress can impact digestive health, including the gallbladder. Practicing stress-relieving techniques such as meditation, mindfulness, or deep breathing exercises helps in managing stress and its adverse effects on the digestive system.

Quality Sleep and Routine:

Establishing a consistent sleep schedule and ensuring adequate rest is crucial. Quality sleep supports overall well-being, including digestive health. Lack of proper sleep may contribute to increased stress levels, which can indirectly affect gallbladder function.

Avoidance of Harmful Habits:

Refraining from harmful habits like smoking, excessive alcohol consumption, and substance abuse is imperative. These habits can contribute to digestive issues and potentially exacerbate gallbladder problems.

Regular Check-ups and Monitoring:

Scheduled visits to healthcare professionals for routine check-ups and discussions about symptoms are essential. This proactive approach aids in early detection and prompt management of potential gallbladder concerns.

Conclusion:

Incorporating these lifestyle changes—maintaining hydration, regular physical activity, stress management, ensuring quality sleep, avoiding harmful habits, and regular medical check-ups—plays a pivotal role in supporting gallbladder function. By embracing these modifications, individuals adopt a proactive stance towards enhancing gallbladder health and promoting overall well-being. However, if we are to summarize, it can be said that the primary changes should indeed revolve around diet. Whether you like it or not, a problematic gallbladder will make you think twice before swallowing any morsel of food. Therefore, focus your main efforts on significant dietary changes and a balanced diet.

HERBAL AND ALTERNATIVE REMEDIES

The allure of herbal remedies often draws individuals seeking natural solutions to health issues, including gallbladder problems. While these remedies have their merits, it's crucial to consider both their potential benefits and the inherent risks associated with such treatments.

The Lengthy Nature of Herbal Treatments:

Herbal treatments often necessitate a prolonged commitment. It can take years to observe significant improvements. However, this duration doesn't always guarantee sustained relief, especially in cases where the body is predisposed to gallstone formation. Despite investing considerable time in herbal treatments, recurrence remains a significant risk, creating a frustrating cycle.

Addressing Root Causes and Behavioral Patterns:

The crux of the matter lies beyond merely ingesting herbal concoctions. It requires a shift in thinking and the management of emotions like anger and aggression. Failure to address these underlying issues can lead to a swift return of gallstones, undermining the efforts invested in herbal treatments.

The Perpetual Nature of Dietary Restrictions:

Moreover, herbal treatments often coincide with stringent dietary regimens. Even post-treatment, maintaining these dietary restrictions becomes a lifelong commitment. Are individuals prepared to embrace such a lifestyle, where dietary limitations persist as constant companions?

Herbs and Their Potential Benefits:

Certain herbs like milk thistle, dandelion root, and turmeric are believed to aid gallbladder health. Milk thistle supports liver function, potentially benefiting bile production. Dandelion root is thought to assist in bile flow. Turmeric, with its anti-inflammatory properties, might aid in alleviating gallbladder discomfort.

«Burdoch» or «burdock» (Arctium) is known for its medicinal properties and is sometimes used in traditional medicine to support digestive health. Its roots can be included in decoctions or infusions, believed to stimulate bile secretion and improve the overall functioning of the gallbladder. However, before using any herbs for medicinal purposes, it's important to consult with a healthcare professional, especially if there are any medical conditions or medications involved, to avoid potential negative interactions.

But there are numerous other herbs upon which healthcare professionals base their treatment systems, often confirming their effectiveness and appropriateness.

Conclusion:

While herbal remedies offer a natural approach to gallbladder issues, their efficacy is variable, and the commitment required extends beyond mere consumption. Addressing emotional triggers, maintaining restrictive diets, and the risk of recurrence demand considerable consideration. The decision to pursue herbal treatments should be made with a realistic understanding of their potential limitations and lifestyle adjustments they may necessitate. Consulting healthcare professionals is crucial for guidance tailored to individual needs and to weigh the benefits against the challenges of such alternative approaches.

Part II: Life After Gallbladder Removal

Understanding Cholecystectomy: Surgery and Recovery

Cholecystectomy, the surgical removal of the gallbladder, stands as a crucial intervention for individuals grappling with gallstone-related issues or gallbladder inflammation. While the mere mention of surgery might induce anxiety, it's essential to understand the procedure's significance and its impact on one's life thereafter.

The gallbladder, though a part of the digestive system, is not indispensable for survival. Its primary function involves storing and concentrating bile produced by the liver. However, gallstones or inflammation can hinder its functionality, leading to severe abdominal pain, nausea, and other discomforting symptoms. In such cases, cholecystectomy becomes a viable solution.

The surgery itself can be performed through laparoscopic or open techniques.

Laparoscopic procedures involve smaller incisions, resulting in quicker recovery times and minimal scarring, while open surgery necessitates a larger incision but might be required in more complex cases.

Post-surgery, patients may experience a brief hospital stay for observation. Recovery periods vary, but most individuals resume normal activities within a few weeks. Dietary adjustments might be recommended initially to accommodate changes in bile flow and aid in digestion.

Recovery after gallbladder removal surgery takes several months. The day after the operation, patients are advised to get up and move independently to prevent adhesions and stagnant processes. Wearing a special abdominal binder is also a mandatory requirement, significantly easing the recovery process. The binder should be worn for three months after the surgery.

Contrary to common belief, life after gallbladder removal often sees an improvement in quality. Relief from recurrent pain and discomfort linked to gallstones often leads to enhanced well-being. However, it's essential to dispel misconceptions about life without a gallbladder. While adaptation is necessary, many individuals lead fulfilling lives by making dietary adjustments and embracing healthy habits.

The fear associated with surgery should not overshadow its benefits. Cholecystectomy, while understandably daunting, is a routine and generally safe procedure. Complications are rare, and the benefits of alleviating gallbladder-related issues often outweigh the risks.

In conclusion, cholecystectomy signifies a resolution to persistent gallbladder issues. It represents an opportunity for improved health and relief from discomfort. Understanding the procedure, its implications, and focusing on post-surgery adjustments contribute to a smoother transition, allowing individuals to lead vibrant lives without the presence of their gallbladder.

Post-Surgery Diet and Nutrition

Laparoscopic gallbladder removal, or cholecystectomy, is considered minimally invasive, less traumatic surgery characterized by a quick recovery period and a low risk of complications.

The main condition for swift recovery and restoration of working capacity is the diet after laparoscopic cholecystectomy. Since the gallbladder, which served as a reservoir for bile and regulated its release into the duodenum, is absent, bile starts to discharge arbitrarily regardless of food intake. This can lead to several unpleasant complications such as cholecystitis, duodenitis, gastritis, colitis, and more.

Therefore, the post-cholecystectomy diet should heavily restrict products that stimulate bile until the bile ducts take over the function of the gallbladder and learn to partially accumulate bile.

Apart from restricting a list of products, the diet after laparoscopic cholecystectomy also involves a special feeding system—fractional eating. This means the patient should eat frequently but in small portions. Since, due to the absence of the gallbladder, bile has no place to accumulate, the quantity expelled through bile ducts might be insufficient to digest significant food portions.

The article further elaborates on the specifics of the post-cholecystectomy diet, the duration it needs to be followed, and provides an example of a healthy menu.

Post-Gallbladder Removal Diet during the Postoperative Period

As mentioned earlier, the diet following gallbladder removal via laparoscopy should be fractional. The patient should consume food 5-6 times a day in small portions. This type of eating after gallbladder removal (laparoscopy) ensures regular bile expulsion from the bile ducts, preventing bile stasis and the formation of stones.

The diet after gallbladder removal (laparoscopy) corresponds to diet table 195 according to Pevzner.

The prohibited list includes fatty meats and fish, concentrated broths, fried, spicy, salty, smoked, pickled, and canned products, fresh pastries, spinach, radishes, onions, garlic, legumes, chocolate, caviar, fresh fruits, carbonated drinks, coffee, strong tea, and alcoholic beverages. Vegetable oil intake is limited to 50 grams per day.

Allowed foods after cholecystectomy include lean meats and fish, light soups, lean broths, porridge, low-fat dairy products, stale bread, baked or lightly boiled fruits.

How Long to Follow the Diet after Gallbladder Removal

The diet after gallbladder removal (laparoscopy) should be followed until the bile ducts partially take on the function of the gallbladder and begin to accumulate and expel bile in necessary amounts for each meal.

Usually, the diet after gallbladder removal (cholecystectomy) is prescribed for at least six months.

For the initial 1.5-2 months after the surgery, it should be strict with maximum restriction of bile-stimulating products. Later, the menu can gradually expand, and for some patients, the diet after gallbladder removal (cholecystectomy) might be prescribed for a year or more.

Healthy Menu after Gallbladder Removal

Usually, a dietitian prepares a sample menu for the patient after gallbladder removal (laparoscopy). In the initial months, it should be strictly followed, and later, it can be slightly diversified.

28-Day Strict Post-Surgery Diet Plan

	Breakfast	Lunch	Snack	Dinner
1 day	Porridge with water, no salt or sugar	Pureed vegetable soup (potatoes, carrots, onions)	Baked apples	Boiled beetroot salad
2 day	Weak black tea with rusks	Pureed vegetable soup	Baked pumpkin	2 slices of baked non-fatty fish
3 day	Porridge with bran	Pureed vegetable soup	Tea or compote with rusks	Mashed potatoes and beetroot salad
4 day	Tea with toast and jam	Pureed fish soup	Baked apples	Boiled buckwheat with a piece of boiled chicken breast
5 day	Porridge with bran	Soup with hard wheat pasta	Tea and a piece of cottage cheese casserole	Rice with steamed chicken meatballs
6 day	Tea with toast and jam	Chicken soup (from chicken breast)	Baked apples and pumpkin	Mashed potatoes and boiled beetroot salad
7 day	Bulgur with apples and cinnamon	Fish and rice soup	Tea with rusks	Buckwheat and boiled chicken breast
8 day	Porridge with berries	Soup with lentils	Tea with toast and a slice of low-fat cheese	Mashed potatoes with baked non-fatty fish
9 day	Greek yogurt with flakes	Noodle soup with chicken breast	Baked apples and pears	Quinoa with sauerkraut
10 day	Bran porridge with raisins	Vegetable soup	Tea with digestive biscuits	Rice with steamed fish cutlet
11 day	Tea with toast and jam	Vegetable soup with broccoli	Rice or buckwheat crackers	Lentils with pickled tomatoes
12 day	Greek yogurt with muesli	Meatball soup	Baked apples	Rice with baked chicken breast
13 day	Porridge with raisins	Vegetable soup	Baked pumpkin	Mashed potatoes and boiled beetroot
14 day	Tea with toast and jam	Chicken breast soup	Rice crackers	Quinoa and lentils stewed with boiled fish

32

	Breakfast	Lunch	Snack	Dinner
15 day	Bran porridge with raisins	Vegetable soup	Tea with digestive biscuits	Rice with steamed fish cutlet
16 day	Weak black tea with rusks	Pureed vegetable soup	Baked pumpkin	2 slices of baked non-fatty fish
17 day	Bulgur with apples and cinnamon	Fish and rice soup	Tea with rusks	Buckwheat and boiled chicken breast
18 day	Porridge with berries	Soup with lentils	Tea with toast and a slice of low-fat cheese	Mashed potatoes with baked non-fatty fish
19 day	Porridge with bran	Soup with hard wheat pasta	Tea and a piece of cottage cheese casserole	Rice with steamed chicken meatballs
20 day	Tea with toast and jam	Pureed fish soup	Baked apples	Boiled buckwheat with a piece of boiled chicken breast
21 day	Porridge with bran	Pureed vegetable soup	Tea or compote with rusks	Mashed potatoes and beetroot salad
22 day	Porridge with water, no salt or sugar	Pureed vegetable soup (potatoes, carrots, onions)	Baked apples	Boiled beetroot salad
23 day	Greek yogurt with muesli	Meatball soup	Baked apples	Rice with baked chicken breast
24 day	Tea with toast and jam	Chicken breast soup	Rice crackers	Quinoa and lentils stewed with boiled fish
25 day	Greek yogurt with flakes	Noodle soup with chicken breast	Baked apples and pears	Quinoa with sauerkraut
26 day	Porridge with raisins	Vegetable soup	Baked pumpkin	Mashed potatoes and boiled beetroot
27 day	Tea with toast and jam	Vegetable soup with broccoli	Rice or buckwheat crackers	Lentils with pickled tomatoes
28 day	Tea with toast and jam	Chicken soup (from chicken breast)	Baked apples and pumpkin	Mashed potatoes and boiled beetroot salad

Important Note: With each passing day after the surgery, you will feel better and better, increasing the temptation to eat something forbidden. Therefore, resist this temptation and adhere to the diet for at least the first three months. Afterward, you can begin expanding your diet, but following a rule: one day, one product. This means that if today you introduced fresh apples into your diet, you should not introduce anything else new. Monitor your body's reaction after introducing new items. If everything is fine, then the next day, you can try something else. However, if you feel any discomfort - stomach spasms or discomfort in the pancreas area, pain, or bloating in the intestines - stop the experiments and return to the diet from a few days ago. In essence, the most important thing is not to rush and not to overindulge.

Part III: Recipes for Preserving Gallbladder Health

Gallbladder-Friendly Recipes

BREAKFASTS

Avocado Toast with Poached Egg

Ingredients:

- 1 ripe avocado
- 2 slices of whole-grain bread
- 2 eggs
- Salt and pepper to taste
- Optional toppings: red pepper flakes, fresh herbs, or a drizzle of olive oil

Instructions:

Prepare the Avocado:

- Cut the avocado in half, remove the pit, and scoop the flesh into a bowl.
- Mash the avocado with a fork until it reaches your desired consistency. Add a pinch of salt and pepper to taste. You can also add a squeeze of lemon juice if desired to prevent browning.

Poach the Eggs:

- Bring a pot of water to a gentle simmer, not a rolling boil. Add a splash of vinegar (optional) to help the egg whites coagulate.
- Crack each egg into a small bowl or ramekin.
- Create a gentle whirlpool in the simmering water using a spoon, then carefully slide the eggs, one at a time, into the center of the whirlpool. This helps the eggs hold their shape.
- Let the eggs cook for about 3-4 minutes for a runny yolk or longer if you prefer a firmer yolk. Use a slotted spoon to carefully remove the poached eggs and place them on a paper towel to drain excess water.

Toast the Bread:

- Toast the slices of whole-grain bread until they reach your preferred level of crispness.

Assemble:

- Spread a generous amount of the mashed avocado onto each slice of toasted bread.
- Carefully place a poached egg on top of the mashed avocado on each slice.
- Season the eggs with a pinch of salt and pepper, and any additional toppings you prefer, such as red pepper flakes, fresh herbs, or a drizzle of olive oil.

Serve:

- Serve the avocado toast with poached eggs immediately while the eggs are still warm.
- Enjoy your delicious and nutritious Avocado Toast with Poached Egg!

Greek Yogurt Parfait

Ingredients:

- Greek yogurt (plain or flavored)
- Fresh berries (strawberries, blueberries, raspberries)
- Granola or muesli
- Honey or maple syrup (optional)
- Nuts or seeds (optional)

Instructions:

Prepare the Ingredients:

- Wash and slice the fresh berries if needed.
- Measure out the desired amount of Greek yogurt and granola or muesli.
- If using nuts or seeds, you can chop or crush them to sprinkle on top.

Layering the Parfait:

- Start by adding a spoonful of Greek yogurt into the bottom of a glass or a bowl, enough to cover the base.
- Next, layer in a handful of fresh berries on top of the yogurt.
- Sprinkle a layer of granola or muesli over the berries.
- Drizzle a small amount of honey or maple syrup over the granola if desired.

Repeat the Layers:

- Repeat the layers by adding another spoonful of Greek yogurt on top of the granola layer.
- Add more fresh berries on top of the yogurt.
- Follow with another layer of granola or muesli.

Finishing Touches:

- Top off the parfait with a final dollop of Greek yogurt.

- Arrange a few fresh berries on the top for a decorative touch.
- If using nuts or seeds, sprinkle them over the final layer of yogurt.

Serve:

- Serve the Greek Yogurt Parfait immediately as a nutritious and satisfying breakfast or snack.

Feel free to adjust the layers and ingredients to suit your preferences. This versatile recipe allows for creativity in layering different fruits, nuts, seeds, or adding a drizzle of your favorite sweetener for added flavor. Enjoy your delightful Greek Yogurt Parfait!

CHIA SEED PUDDING

Ingredients:

- 1/4 cup chia seeds
- 1 cup milk of choice (almond milk, coconut milk, or any other preferred milk)
- Sweetener (honey, maple syrup, agave nectar) - optional
- Vanilla extract - optional
- Toppings: Fresh fruits, nuts, or granola (optional)

Instructions:

Mix the Chia Seeds and Milk:

- In a bowl or a jar, combine the chia seeds and milk in a ratio of 1:4 (for example, 1/4 cup chia seeds to 1 cup milk). Stir well to combine.

Add Sweetener and Flavor (Optional):

- If desired, add sweetener to the mixture according to your taste preferences. You can use honey, maple syrup, or agave nectar. Start with about a teaspoon and adjust to taste.
- Optional: Add a splash of vanilla extract for extra flavor. Mix well to

incorporate.

Let it Sit and Stir:

- Once everything is thoroughly mixed, cover the bowl or jar and let it sit for about 5-10 minutes.
- After the initial resting time, stir the mixture again to prevent the chia seeds from clumping together.

Refrigerate Overnight (or for at least a few hours):

- Cover the bowl or jar and refrigerate the chia seed mixture for at least 3-4 hours, ideally overnight. This allows the chia seeds to absorb the liquid and form a pudding-like consistency.

Check and Stir Again:

- After the resting period, check the pudding. It should have thickened significantly. Stir it well to break up any clumps and ensure an even texture.

Serve and Add Toppings:

- Spoon the chia seed pudding into serving bowls or jars.
- Add your favorite toppings such as fresh fruits (sliced berries, banana, mango), nuts (almonds, walnuts), or granola for extra texture and flavor.

Enjoy:

- Serve the chia seed pudding immediately as a healthy breakfast or snack option.

This Chia Seed Pudding is versatile, allowing for various modifications in terms of sweetness, flavorings, and toppings to suit your preferences. Experiment with different combinations to create your perfect chia seed pudding!

Smoked Salmon Bagel

Ingredients:

- 1 whole-grain bagel, sliced in half horizontally
- 3-4 ounces of smoked salmon slices (adjust to preference)
- 2-3 tablespoons of cream cheese (softened)
- 1 tablespoon of capers (drained)
- 1/4 red onion, thinly sliced
- Optional: Lemon wedges, fresh dill, or arugula for garnish

Instructions:

Prepare the Bagel:

- Slice the whole-grain bagel horizontally and toast it lightly if desired, achieving a golden crispness without making it overly crunchy.

Spread Cream Cheese:

- Spread a generous amount of softened cream cheese on both halves of the bagel. Ensure even coverage to the edges.

Layer Smoked Salmon:

- Lay the smoked salmon slices evenly on the bottom half of the bagel. Overlapping the slices slightly ensures complete coverage.

Add Capers and Red Onion:

- Sprinkle the drained capers evenly over the smoked salmon layer. They provide a tangy burst of flavor.
- Place the thinly sliced red onion rings on top of the capers, evenly distributed across the salmon layer.

Optional Garnish:

- Optionally, serve with fresh lemon wedges on the side for a tangy touch. Squeezing lemon juice over the salmon adds a refreshing zing.
- For additional flavor or presentation, garnish with fresh dill sprigs or a few arugula leaves on top.

Assemble the Bagel:

- Gently place the top half of the bagel over the assembled layers, creating a complete sandwich.

Serve:

- Serve the Smoked Salmon Bagel immediately, either open-faced or closed, according to personal preference.

This detailed guide ensures you can assemble a Smoked Salmon Bagel with precision, balancing the creamy richness of the cream cheese, the savory smoked salmon, the briny pop of capers, and the zesty crunch of red onions. Adjust the quantities of each ingredient to suit your taste preferences, and savor this delightful breakfast or brunch option!

Egg and Veggie Scramble

Ingredients:

- 2-3 eggs
- Handful of spinach leaves (chopped)
- 4-5 mushrooms (sliced)
- 1/2 bell pepper (diced)
- Salt and pepper to taste
- Olive oil or butter for cooking

Instructions:

Prep the Veggies:

- Wash the spinach leaves thoroughly and chop them.

- Slice the mushrooms and dice the bell pepper into small pieces.

Sauté the Vegetables:

- Heat a non-stick skillet over medium heat and add a splash of olive oil or a small knob of butter.
- Add the chopped spinach to the skillet and sauté for about a minute until it starts to wilt.
- Then, add the sliced mushrooms and diced bell pepper to the skillet. Sauté the vegetables together until they soften and release their moisture, usually for about 3-4 minutes.

Scramble the Eggs:

- In a bowl, crack the eggs and whisk them until they're well combined. Season with a pinch of salt and pepper.
- Push the sautéed vegetables to one side of the skillet and pour the beaten eggs into the cleared space.

Combine and Cook:

- Allow the eggs to sit for a few seconds until they start to set at the edges.
- Using a spatula, gently scramble the eggs, moving them around to combine them with the sautéed vegetables. Continue stirring occasionally until the eggs are cooked to your preferred consistency, ensuring they're no longer runny.

Season and Serve:

- Taste the scramble and adjust the seasoning with more salt and pepper if needed.
- Once the eggs are cooked through, transfer the Egg and Veggie Scramble to a plate.

Garnish (Optional):

- You can garnish the scramble with some fresh herbs like parsley or chives if desired for extra flavor and presentation.

Serve Warm:

- Serve the Egg and Veggie Scramble immediately while it's still hot and enjoy a nutritious and delicious breakfast!

This Egg and Veggie Scramble offers a delightful combination of eggs packed with protein and a variety of sautéed vegetables, making it a healthy and satisfying breakfast option. Adjust the quantities of veggies and seasoning according to your taste preferences.

Coconut Mango Smoothie

Ingredients:

- 1 cup coconut milk
- 1 cup frozen mango chunks
- 1/2 cup Greek yogurt
- 1 tablespoon honey or agave syrup (optional, adjust to taste)
- Ice cubes (optional, for a thicker consistency)

Instructions:

Prepare the Ingredients:

- Measure out the coconut milk, frozen mango chunks, Greek yogurt, and honey or agave syrup.

Combine Ingredients in Blender:

- In a blender, add the coconut milk as the base.
- Add the frozen mango chunks on top of the coconut milk.
- Spoon in the Greek yogurt.
- Optionally, include the honey or agave syrup for added sweetness.

Blend Until Smooth:

- Secure the blender lid tightly and start blending the ingredients on high speed.

- Blend for about 1-2 minutes or until all the ingredients are completely smooth and well combined. If you prefer a thicker consistency, you can add a handful of ice cubes and blend again until smooth.

Taste and Adjust:

- Taste the smoothie and adjust the sweetness by adding more honey or agave syrup if needed. Blend again briefly to incorporate any additional ingredients.

Serve:

- Pour the Coconut Mango Smoothie into glasses.
- Optionally, garnish with a slice of fresh mango or a sprinkle of shredded coconut on top for presentation.

Enjoy:

- Sip and relish this delightful Coconut Mango Smoothie immediately as a refreshing breakfast beverage or a revitalizing snack.

This smoothie offers a tropical twist with the combination of creamy coconut milk, sweet frozen mango, and the tanginess of Greek yogurt. It's not only a delicious treat but also a nutritious choice packed with vitamins and minerals. Adjust the sweetness or consistency according to your taste preferences for a perfect blend every time!

QUINOA BREAKFAST BOWL

Ingredients:

- 1 cup cooked quinoa
- 1 ripe avocado
- 1-2 eggs (depending on preference)
- 2 tablespoons crumbled feta cheese
- Salt and pepper to taste

- Olive oil for frying the egg (optional)

Instructions:

Prepare the Quinoa:

- If the quinoa isn't cooked already, follow the package instructions to prepare 1 cup of cooked quinoa. Fluff it with a fork once cooked.

Slice the Avocado:

- Cut the ripe avocado in half, remove the pit, and slice the avocado into thin pieces. Set aside.

Cook the Eggs:

- In a non-stick skillet, heat a small amount of olive oil over medium heat (optional). Crack the egg(s) into the skillet.
- Cook the egg(s) to your desired level of doneness—frying until the whites are set but the yolk is still slightly runny usually takes around 3-4 minutes.

Assemble the Quinoa Breakfast Bowl:

- In a bowl, add a serving of cooked quinoa as the base.
- Top the quinoa with the sliced avocado, arranging it neatly around the edges or however you prefer.
- Carefully place the cooked egg(s) on top of the quinoa and avocado.

Sprinkle Feta and Season:

- Sprinkle the crumbled feta cheese over the entire bowl.
- Season the dish with a pinch of salt and pepper to taste.

Serve and Enjoy:

- Your Quinoa Breakfast Bowl is now ready to enjoy! Serve it immediately while the egg is warm and the ingredients are fresh.

This breakfast bowl offers a nutritious and hearty meal with the protein-rich quinoa, creamy avocado, the richness of the fried egg, and the savory touch of feta cheese. It's a balanced breakfast option that provides essential nutrients and is customizable based on personal preferences. Adjust the quantities of ingredients as desired and savor this delightful dish!

ALMOND BUTTER BANANA TOAST

Ingredients:

- 1-2 slices of whole-grain bread
- Almond butter
- 1 ripe banana, thinly sliced

Instructions:

Toast the Bread:

- Toast one or two slices of whole-grain bread until they reach your desired level of crispness.

Spread Almond Butter:

- Once the toast is ready, spread a generous layer of almond butter on each slice. Ensure even coverage from edge to edge.

Add Banana Slices:

- Thinly slice a ripe banana and place the banana slices on top of the almond butter layer. You can arrange them in a single layer or slightly overlap them.

Optional Toppings (If Desired):

- If you want to add extra flavor or texture, you can sprinkle a pinch of cinnamon, chia seeds, or a drizzle of honey over the banana slices.

Serve and Enjoy:

- Your Almond Butter Banana Toast is ready to be enjoyed! It's a delicious combination of nutty almond butter and the natural sweetness of bananas, perfect for a quick and satisfying breakfast or snack.

Frittata with Spinach and Feta

Ingredients:

- 6 large eggs
- 2 cups fresh spinach leaves
- 1/2 cup crumbled feta cheese
- 1/2 cup cherry tomatoes, halved
- Salt and pepper to taste
- Olive oil for cooking

Instructions:

Preheat Oven and Prepare Ingredients:

- Preheat your oven to 350°F (175°C).
- Wash the spinach leaves and cherry tomatoes. Pat them dry with a paper towel. Crumble the feta cheese if not already crumbled.

Sauté the Spinach:

- Heat a little olive oil in an oven-safe skillet over medium heat. Add the spinach leaves and sauté until they wilt and shrink in size, usually for about 2-3 minutes. Season with salt and pepper to taste.

Whisk the Eggs:

- In a bowl, whisk the eggs until well combined. Season with a pinch of salt and pepper.

Assemble the Frittata:

- Once the spinach is cooked, evenly distribute it across the skillet.
- Pour the whisked eggs over the spinach, ensuring they cover the entire skillet.
- Sprinkle crumbled feta cheese evenly over the egg and spinach mixture.
- Place the halved cherry tomatoes on top of the mixture.

Bake the Frittata:

- Transfer the skillet to the preheated oven and bake for about 15-20 minutes, or until the eggs are set and the frittata turns slightly golden on top.

Serve Warm:

- Once done, remove the skillet from the oven. Allow it to cool for a few minutes before slicing.
- Serve the Frittata with Spinach and Feta warm, either as a breakfast option or a delightful brunch dish!

These recipes offer a fantastic variety—one a quick and flavorful toast and the other a more elaborate and savory baked egg dish—both perfect for different occasions or preferences. Adjust seasoning and ingredients as desired for your ideal taste!

Oatmeal with Almond Butter

Ingredients:

- 1/2 cup steel-cut oats
- 1 cup water or milk (almond milk, dairy milk, etc.)
- 1 tablespoon almond butter
- Sliced almonds (for topping)
- Honey or maple syrup (optional, for drizzling)

Instructions:

Cook the Oats:

- In a saucepan, bring water or milk to a boil.
- Add the steel-cut oats, reduce the heat to low, and simmer for about 20-25 minutes, stirring occasionally, until the oats are tender and have absorbed most of the liquid.

Serve the Oatmeal:

- Once the oats are cooked to your desired consistency, transfer them to a serving bowl.

Top with Almond Butter and Almonds:

- Dollop a tablespoon of almond butter onto the cooked oats.
- Sprinkle a handful of sliced almonds on top of the almond butter.

Optional Sweetener:

- Drizzle a bit of honey or maple syrup over the oatmeal for added sweetness, if desired.

Stir and Enjoy:

- Gently stir the almond butter, almonds, and sweetener into the oatmeal.
- Your delicious and nutritious Oatmeal with Almond Butter is ready to enjoy!

Egg and Avocado Breakfast Burrito

Ingredients:

- Whole-grain tortilla
- 2-3 large eggs, scrambled
- 1 ripe avocado, sliced
- Salsa (as desired)

Instructions:

Prepare the Eggs:

- Scramble the eggs in a skillet over medium heat until cooked through.

Assemble the Burrito:

- Place the scrambled eggs in the center of a whole-grain tortilla.

Add Avocado and Salsa:

- Arrange slices of ripe avocado on top of the eggs.
- Add a spoonful of salsa over the avocado and eggs.

Fold the Burrito:

- Fold the sides of the tortilla inward and roll it up tightly, creating a burrito shape.

Serve:

- Your Egg and Avocado Breakfast Burrito is ready to be served! It's a delightful combination of protein-packed eggs and creamy avocado in a convenient handheld form.

BLUEBERRY ALMOND PANCAKES

Ingredients:

- Whole-grain pancake mix (follow package instructions for batter)
- Fresh blueberries
- Chopped almonds

Instructions:

Prepare Pancake Batter:

- Follow the instructions on the whole-grain pancake mix to prepare the batter. Ensure it's smooth and well-mixed.

Add Blueberries and Almonds:

- Gently fold fresh blueberries and chopped almonds into the pancake batter.

Cook Pancakes:

- Heat a non-stick skillet or griddle over medium heat and lightly grease it.
- Pour portions of the pancake batter onto the skillet to form pancakes.

Cook Until Golden:

- Cook the pancakes until bubbles form on the surface, then flip and cook the other side until both sides are golden brown.

Serve Warm:

- Serve the Blueberry Almond Pancakes while they're warm and enjoy the delightful combination of fresh blueberries and crunchy almonds in every bite!

Salmon Breakfast Hash:

Ingredients:

- 1 salmon fillet
- 1 cup diced sweet potatoes
- 1/2 cup diced onions

- 1/2 cup diced bell peppers (any color)
- Salt, pepper, and preferred seasonings
- Olive oil for cooking

Instructions:

Prepare the Salmon:

- Season the salmon fillet with salt, pepper, and your choice of preferred seasonings.
- In a skillet over medium heat, add a bit of olive oil and pan-sear the salmon for about 3-4 minutes per side until cooked through. Once done, remove the salmon from the skillet and set it aside.

Cook the Hash:

- In the same skillet, add a little more olive oil if needed.
- Add diced sweet potatoes and cook for about 5-7 minutes until they start to soften.
- Stir in the diced onions and bell peppers, and continue cooking until all the vegetables are tender and slightly caramelized.

Combine and Serve:

- Break the pan-seared salmon into smaller chunks and add it to the cooked hash.
- Gently mix everything together and season to taste with additional salt and pepper if needed.
- Your flavorful Salmon Breakfast Hash is ready to be served!

MUSHROOM AND SPINACH OMELETTE:

Ingredients:

- 3 large eggs
- Handful of fresh spinach leaves
- Sliced mushrooms

- Shredded Swiss cheese
- Salt, pepper, and preferred seasonings
- Olive oil or butter for cooking

Instructions:

Prepare the Fillings:

- Sauté the sliced mushrooms in a skillet over medium heat until they are golden brown. Remove and set aside.
- In the same skillet, add a bit of olive oil or butter and sauté the fresh spinach until wilted. Remove and set aside.

Whisk the Eggs:

- Crack the eggs into a bowl, season with salt, pepper, and preferred seasonings. Whisk until well-beaten.

Cook the Omelette:

- Heat the skillet over medium heat and add a little more oil or butter if needed.
- Pour the beaten eggs into the skillet, swirling to ensure even distribution.

Add Fillings and Cheese:

- Once the eggs begin to set, add the sautéed mushrooms and wilted spinach on one half of the omelette.
- Sprinkle shredded Swiss cheese over the fillings.

Fold and Serve:

- Use a spatula to fold the other half of the omelette over the fillings, creating a half-moon shape.
- Cook for another minute until the cheese melts.
- Your Mushroom and Spinach Omelette is ready to be served!

Coconut Flour Pancakes

Ingredients:

- 1/4 cup coconut flour
- 4 eggs
- 1/4 cup milk of your choice (almond milk, coconut milk, etc.)
- 1/2 teaspoon baking powder
- Optional: sweetener like honey or maple syrup (to taste)
- Butter or oil for cooking
- Greek yogurt and fresh fruit for serving

Instructions:

Mix the Batter:

- In a bowl, whisk together the eggs, coconut flour, milk, baking powder, and optional sweetener until a smooth batter forms. Let it sit for a few minutes to allow the coconut flour to absorb the liquid.

Cook the Pancakes:

- Heat a skillet or griddle over medium heat and lightly grease it with butter or oil.
- Pour small portions of the batter onto the skillet to form pancakes. Cook for 2-3 minutes per side, until golden brown.

Serve:

- Stack the coconut flour pancakes on a plate.
- Serve with a dollop of Greek yogurt and fresh fruit of your choice, such as berries or sliced bananas, on top.

Nutty Banana Smoothie

Ingredients:

- 1 ripe banana
- 1 cup almond milk
- 1-2 tablespoons peanut butter
- Pinch of cinnamon

Instructions:

Blend the Ingredients:

- In a blender, combine the ripe banana (broken into chunks), almond milk, peanut butter, and a pinch of cinnamon.

Blend Until Smooth:

- Blend the ingredients until you achieve a smooth and creamy consistency.

Serve:

- Pour the nutty banana smoothie into a glass.
- Optionally, sprinkle a bit of cinnamon on top for garnish.
- Enjoy the creamy and flavorful smoothie!

Sweet Potato Breakfast Skillet

Ingredients:

- 1 large sweet potato, peeled and diced
- 1/2 onion, diced
- Turkey sausage (precooked or cooked and crumbled)
- 1-2 eggs (per serving)
- Salt, pepper, and preferred seasonings

- Olive oil for cooking

Instructions:

Sauté the Sweet Potatoes and Onions:

- Heat olive oil in a skillet over medium heat.
- Add diced sweet potatoes and onions, sauté until they start to brown and become tender.

Add Turkey Sausage:

- Add the precooked or crumbled turkey sausage to the skillet and continue cooking until everything is heated through.

Fry the Eggs:

- Create wells in the skillet and crack eggs into them.
- Cover the skillet and cook until the eggs are done to your preference.

Serve:

- Once the eggs are cooked, season the skillet with salt, pepper, or any preferred seasonings.
- Serve the Sweet Potato Breakfast Skillet hot, with the fried eggs on top of the sautéed mixture.

These recipes offer a variety of flavors and textures, from fluffy pancakes to a hearty skillet breakfast and a creamy smoothie. Enjoy creating and indulging in these delicious breakfast options!

ALMOND FLOUR WAFFLES

Ingredients:

- 1 1/2 cups almond flour
- 3 eggs
- 1/4 cup milk of your choice

- 1 tablespoon melted butter or oil
- 1/2 teaspoon baking powder
- Optional: sweetener like honey or maple syrup (to taste)
- Greek yogurt and sliced strawberries for serving

Instructions:

Prepare the Batter:

- In a mixing bowl, whisk together the almond flour, eggs, milk, melted butter or oil, baking powder, and optional sweetener until smooth.

Cook the Waffles:

- Preheat your waffle iron and lightly grease it with butter or oil.
- Pour enough batter onto the waffle iron to cover the griddle and cook according to the manufacturer's instructions until golden and crispy.

Serve:

- Plate the waffles and serve with a dollop of Greek yogurt and fresh sliced strawberries on top or on the side.

Egg and Spinach Breakfast Wrap

Ingredients:

- Whole-grain wrap or tortilla
- 2-3 eggs, scrambled
- Handful of fresh spinach leaves
- Shredded cheese
- Salt, pepper, and preferred seasonings
- Olive oil or butter for cooking

Instructions:

Prepare the Fillings:
- In a skillet over medium heat, sauté the fresh spinach leaves until they wilt. Remove and set aside.
- Scramble the eggs in the same skillet, seasoning them with salt, pepper, and any preferred seasonings.

Assemble the Wrap:
- Place the scrambled eggs and sautéed spinach onto the center of the whole-grain wrap.
- Sprinkle shredded cheese over the eggs and spinach.

Fold the Wrap:
- Fold the sides of the wrap over the fillings and roll it tightly, creating a wrap shape.

Serve:
- Optionally, lightly toast the assembled wrap in a skillet for a minute or two for added crispness.
- Slice the wrap in half diagonally and serve.

Peanut Butter Overnight Oats

Ingredients:

- 1/2 cup rolled oats
- 1/2 cup almond milk (or any preferred milk)
- 1-2 tablespoons peanut butter
- Sliced bananas

Instructions:

Mix the Ingredients:

- In a jar or bowl, combine the rolled oats, almond milk, and peanut butter. Stir until well-mixed.

Add Sliced Bananas:

- Add sliced bananas into the mixture and stir gently to combine.

Refrigerate Overnight:

- Cover the jar or bowl and refrigerate overnight, allowing the oats to soften and absorb the liquid.

Serve:

- The next morning, give the overnight oats a stir, and they're ready to be enjoyed cold. Optionally, you can heat them up before serving.

These breakfast options offer a delightful array of flavors, textures, and nutrition, from the nutty waffles to the convenient and tasty overnight oats and the wholesome breakfast wrap. Enjoy these delicious and fulfilling meals!

LUNCHES

Grilled Chicken Salad:

Ingredients:

- Grilled chicken breast slices
- Mixed greens
- Cherry tomatoes
- Cucumber
- Lemon-herb dressing

Instructions:

1. Grill the Chicken: Season and grill chicken breast slices until cooked through. Let them rest before slicing.
2. Prepare the Salad Base: Wash and chop mixed greens, cherry tomatoes, and cucumber.
3. Assemble the Salad: Arrange mixed greens on a plate. Top with grilled chicken, tomatoes, and cucumber.
4. Dress the Salad: Drizzle with lemon-herb dressing before serving. Toss gently.

Quinoa Salad:

Ingredients:

- Cooked quinoa
- Diced bell peppers
- Cucumbers
- Tomatoes
- Lemon-tahini dressing

Instructions:

1. Prepare Quinoa: Cook and cool quinoa as per package instructions.
2. Chop Vegetables: Dice bell peppers, cucumbers, and tomatoes.

3. Combine Ingredients: Mix quinoa with diced vegetables in a bowl.
4. Add Dressing: Drizzle lemon-tahini dressing over the salad. Toss gently to combine.

Tuna Lettuce Wraps:

Ingredients:

- Canned tuna
- Greek yogurt
- Celery
- Onions
- Lettuce leaves

Instructions:

1. Prepare Tuna Filling: Mix drained tuna with Greek yogurt, chopped celery, and onions.
2. Assemble Wraps: Spoon tuna mixture onto lettuce leaves.
3. Wrap & Serve: Roll lettuce leaves around the filling to form wraps. Serve immediately.

These recipes offer diverse and healthy lunch options suitable for a gallbladder-friendly diet. Adjust quantities and seasonings based on preferences.

Mediterranean Chickpea Salad

Ingredients:

- 1 can chickpeas (drained and rinsed)
- Feta cheese (crumbled)
- Cherry tomatoes (halved)
- Olives (pitted and sliced)
- Red onion (finely chopped)
- Light vinaigrette (olive oil, lemon juice, herbs)

Instructions:

Prepare Ingredients:

- Rinse and drain chickpeas. Cut cherry tomatoes and red onion.

Mix Salad:

- In a bowl, combine chickpeas, cherry tomatoes, olives, red onion, and crumbled feta cheese.

Add Dressing:

- Drizzle the light vinaigrette over the salad. Toss gently to coat evenly. Refrigerate before serving.

Veggie Stir-Fry

Ingredients:

- Colorful bell peppers (sliced)
- Broccoli florets
- Snap peas
- Tofu or chicken (diced)
- Soy sauce or teriyaki sauce
- Brown rice (cooked)

Instructions:

Stir-Fry Vegetables:

- In a pan, stir-fry bell peppers, broccoli, and snap peas until tender-crisp.

Cook Protein:

- If using tofu or chicken, cook separately until browned.

Combine Ingredients:

- Add the cooked protein to the vegetable mix. Stir in soy sauce or teriyaki sauce. Serve over brown rice.

Turkey and Avocado Wrap

Ingredients:

- Sliced turkey breast
- Ripe avocado (mashed)
- Lettuce leaves
- Tomato slices
- Whole-grain wrap

Instructions:

Prepare Ingredients:

- Slice tomato and gather lettuce leaves.

Assemble Wrap:

- Lay out the whole-grain wrap. Spread mashed avocado evenly on the wrap.

Add Fillings:

- Place sliced turkey, lettuce leaves, and tomato slices over the avocado.

Roll Wrap:

- Roll the ingredients tightly inside the wrap. Cut in half if desired. Serve immediately.

Vegetable Soup

Ingredients:

- Carrots (sliced)
- Celery (chopped)
- Onions (diced)
- Spinach leaves
- Vegetable broth
- Seasonings (salt, pepper, herbs as preferred)

Instructions:

Prepare Ingredients:

- Chop carrots, celery, and onions. Rinse spinach leaves.

Cook Soup:

- In a pot, heat vegetable broth. Add carrots, celery, and onions. Simmer until vegetables are tender.

Add Spinach:

- Stir in spinach leaves and cook for a few more minutes until wilted. Season with preferred herbs, salt, and pepper.

Serve:

- Ladle the soup into bowls. Optionally, garnish with fresh herbs.

Egg Salad Lettuce Cups

Ingredients:

- Hard-boiled eggs (chopped)
- Greek yogurt

- Mustard
- Chopped herbs (parsley, chives)
- Lettuce leaves

Instructions:

Prepare Egg Salad:
- Mix chopped hard-boiled eggs with Greek yogurt, mustard, and chopped herbs. Season as desired.

Assemble Lettuce Cups:
- Spoon the egg salad into individual lettuce leaves, forming cups.

Serve:
- Arrange the lettuce cups on a plate and serve.

Roasted Veggie Quinoa Bowl

Ingredients:

- Zucchini (sliced)
- Eggplant (cubed)
- Bell peppers (sliced)
- Quinoa (cooked)
- Lemon-herb dressing
- Olive oil
- Seasonings (salt, pepper, herbs)

Instructions:

Roast Vegetables:

- Preheat oven. Toss zucchini, eggplant, and bell peppers with olive oil, salt, and pepper. Roast until tender.

Prepare Quinoa:

- Cook quinoa according to package instructions.

Assemble Bowl:

- Place the roasted vegetables on a bed of cooked quinoa. Drizzle with lemon-herb dressing.

Serve:

- Enjoy this flavorful and nutritious roasted vegetable quinoa bowl!

Cauliflower Rice Stir-Fry

Ingredients:

- Cauliflower rice
- Mixed vegetables (bell peppers, broccoli, carrots, etc.)
- Lean protein (shrimp, tofu, chicken)
- Soy sauce or preferred stir-fry sauce
- Garlic, ginger (optional)
- Olive oil

Instructions:

Prepare Ingredients:

- If using fresh cauliflower, pulse it in a food processor to create cauliflower rice. Chop mixed vegetables and protein into bite-sized pieces.

Stir-Fry:

- Heat olive oil in a pan. Add garlic and ginger (if using) and sauté briefly.
- Add cauliflower rice, mixed vegetables, and lean protein. Stir-fry until cooked but still slightly crisp.

Season:

- Drizzle with soy sauce or preferred stir-fry sauce, tossing to coat evenly.

Serve:

- Plate the cauliflower rice stir-fry and enjoy!

SALMON SALAD

Ingredients:

- Baked or grilled salmon
- Mixed greens
- Cucumbers (sliced)
- Lemon dressing (lemon juice, olive oil, salt, pepper)

Instructions:

Prepare Salmon:

- Bake or grill salmon until cooked. Flake into bite-sized pieces.

Assemble Salad:

- Toss mixed greens and sliced cucumbers in a bowl.
- Add the flaked salmon to the greens.

Dressing:

- Whisk together lemon juice, olive oil, salt, and pepper for a light dressing.

Combine:

- Drizzle the lemon dressing over the salmon and greens, gently tossing to combine.

Serve:

- Plate the salmon salad and serve as a refreshing and nutritious meal.

Zucchini Noodles with Pesto

Ingredients:

- Zucchini (spiralized into noodles)
- Cherry tomatoes
- Homemade pesto sauce (basil, pine nuts, garlic, olive oil, parmesan cheese)

Instructions:

Prepare Ingredients:

- Spiralize zucchini into noodle shapes. Halve cherry tomatoes.

Make Pesto:

- Blend basil, pine nuts, garlic, olive oil, and parmesan cheese until smooth to create the pesto sauce.

Cook Zucchini Noodles:

- In a pan, lightly sauté zucchini noodles until just tender.

Combine:

- Toss the zucchini noodles with the homemade pesto sauce and cherry tomatoes.

Serve:

- Plate the zucchini noodles with pesto, garnish with extra basil or parmesan if desired, and serve.

Black Bean Tacos

Ingredients:

- Black beans (cooked)
- Sautéed onions and bell peppers
- Whole-grain tortillas
- Shredded cheese (optional)
- Salsa, guacamole (optional)

Instructions:

Prepare Ingredients:

- Cook black beans and sauté onions and bell peppers until tender.

Assemble Tacos:

- Warm whole-grain tortillas. Layer black beans, sautéed onions, and bell peppers onto the tortillas.
- Optionally, add a sprinkle of shredded cheese.

Serve:

- Serve the black bean tacos with salsa or guacamole if desired, and enjoy a flavorful taco meal!

Feel free to personalize these recipes with your preferred seasonings and toppings for a delightful lunch experience!

Greek Quinoa Stuffed Peppers

Ingredients:

- 1 cup quinoa
- 1/2 cup crumbled feta cheese
- 1 cup diced tomatoes
- 1/2 cup sliced olives
- 4 bell peppers

Instructions:

Prepare Ingredients:

- Cook quinoa according to package instructions.
- In a mixing bowl, combine cooked quinoa, crumbled feta cheese, diced tomatoes, and sliced olives.

Prepare Bell Peppers:

- Preheat the oven to 375°F (190°C).
- Cut the tops off the bell peppers and remove seeds and membranes.
- Stuff each bell pepper evenly with the quinoa mixture.

Bake:

- Place the stuffed bell peppers in a baking dish.
- Bake for about 25-30 minutes until the peppers are tender and slightly charred.

Serve:

- Serve the Greek quinoa stuffed peppers warm, garnished with fresh herbs if desired.

Lentil Soup

Ingredients:

- 1 cup lentils, rinsed
- 2 carrots, chopped
- 1 onion, chopped
- 2 celery stalks, chopped
- 4 cups vegetable broth
- Salt, pepper, and herbs to taste

Instructions:

Prepare Ingredients:

- Rinse the lentils thoroughly and set them aside.
- In a pot, sauté chopped onions, carrots, and celery until softened.

Cook Lentils:

- Add the rinsed lentils to the pot along with vegetable broth.
- Season with salt, pepper, and herbs.

Simmer:

- Bring the mixture to a boil, then reduce the heat and simmer for 25-30 minutes until the lentils are tender.

Serve:

- Ladle the lentil soup into bowls and serve hot, optionally garnished with fresh parsley.

Grilled Veggie Sandwich

Ingredients:

- 1 eggplant, sliced
- 1 zucchini, sliced
- 1 red pepper, sliced
- Hummus
- Whole-grain bread slices

Instructions:

Grill Veggies:

- Preheat a grill or grill pan over medium heat.
- Grill the eggplant, zucchini, and red pepper slices until tender and grill marks appear, for about 3-4 minutes per side.

Prepare Sandwich:

- Spread a layer of hummus on one side of each whole-grain bread slice.
- Layer the grilled vegetables between the bread slices to assemble the sandwiches.

Grill (Optional):

- Optionally, place the assembled sandwiches on the grill for a minute or two for a warm, toasty sandwich.

Serve:

- Cut the grilled veggie sandwiches in half and serve them warm.

TOFU LETTUCE WRAPS

Ingredients:

- 1 block firm tofu, drained and cubed
- 1 can water chestnuts, drained and chopped
- 1 cup mushrooms, diced
- Asian spices (like soy sauce, ginger, garlic)
- Lettuce leaves for wrapping

Instructions:

Prepare Tofu and Veggies:

- In a skillet over medium heat, add a bit of oil and stir-fry the tofu cubes until lightly browned. Set aside.
- In the same skillet, stir-fry the water chestnuts and diced mushrooms until tender.
- Add the Asian spices (soy sauce, ginger, garlic, etc.) for flavor.

Combine Ingredients:

- Mix the cooked tofu with the stir-fried vegetables in the skillet. Stir to combine and allow the flavors to meld.

Assemble Lettuce Wraps:

- Spoon the tofu and vegetable mixture into individual lettuce leaves, creating wraps.

Serve:

- Arrange the tofu lettuce wraps on a plate and serve them as a light, flavorful dish.

Chickpea Spinach Salad

Ingredients:

- 1 can chickpeas (garbanzo beans), drained and rinsed
- Fresh spinach leaves
- Diced cucumbers
- Lemon-tahini dressing (made with tahini, lemon juice, garlic, olive oil)
- Instructions:

Prepare Salad:

- In a mixing bowl, combine the chickpeas, fresh spinach leaves, and diced cucumbers.

Dress the Salad:

- Drizzle the lemon-tahini dressing over the salad mixture. Toss gently to coat the ingredients evenly.

Serve:

- Serve the chickpea spinach salad in bowls, garnishing with additional lemon slices if desired.

Turkey and Spinach Quiche

Ingredients:

- 1 pound ground turkey
- Fresh spinach leaves (as desired)
- 1 cup low-fat cheese, shredded
- 4-5 eggs
- Salt, pepper, and preferred spices for seasoning

Instructions:

Prepare Ingredients:

- Preheat the oven to 375°F (190°C).
- In a skillet, brown the ground turkey over medium heat, seasoning it with salt, pepper, and preferred spices. Drain excess fat if needed.
- In a mixing bowl, beat the eggs and then mix in the fresh spinach leaves (chopped) and low-fat cheese.

Assemble Quiche:

- Grease a pie dish and spread the cooked ground turkey evenly at the bottom.
- Pour the egg, spinach, and cheese mixture over the turkey, ensuring even coverage.

Bake:

- Place the quiche in the preheated oven and bake for approximately 30-35 minutes or until the quiche is set and lightly browned on top.

Serve:

- Allow the quiche to cool slightly before slicing and serving.

Cucumber and Avocado Sushi Rolls

Ingredients:

- Sushi rice (prepared as per package instructions)
- Nori (seaweed) sheets
- 1 cucumber, julienned
- Avocado slices
- Crab sticks (or imitation crab)
- Bamboo sushi mat

Instructions:

Prepare Ingredients:

- Lay a nori sheet on the bamboo sushi mat.
- Spread a thin layer of prepared sushi rice evenly over the nori sheet, leaving a small space at the top.

Add Fillings:

- Place julienned cucumber, avocado slices, and crab sticks along the bottom edge of the rice-covered nori sheet.

Roll the Sushi:

- Using the bamboo mat, start rolling the nori sheet tightly, beginning from the bottom edge and rolling towards the top.
- Seal the edges by applying a small amount of water along the top edge of the nori sheet.

Slice and Serve:

- Use a sharp knife to cut the roll into individual sushi pieces.
- Serve the cucumber and avocado sushi rolls with soy sauce but without pickled ginger.

SNACKS

Apple Slices with Almond Butter

Ingredients:

- Apples: 2 medium, sliced
- Almond butter: 1/4 cup

Instructions:

Preparing Apples:

- Wash and slice the apples into wedges or rounds.

Serving:

- Dip apple slices into almond butter before consuming.

Benefits:

- Apples: Rich in fiber and antioxidants, apples can aid in digestion and promote heart health.
- Almond Butter: Provides healthy fats, protein, and vitamin E, which supports skin health and offers sustained energy.

Greek Yogurt with Berries

Ingredients:

- Greek yogurt: 1 cup
- Mixed berries: 1/2 cup (strawberries, blueberries, raspberries)

Instructions:

Assembling:

- Place Greek yogurt in a bowl.
- Top with mixed berries.

Benefits:

- Greek Yogurt: High in protein and probiotics, Greek yogurt supports gut health and provides calcium for strong bones.
- Berries: Packed with antioxidants and vitamins, berries offer anti-inflammatory properties and support immune function.

Carrot Sticks with Hummus:

Ingredients:

- Carrots: 2-3 medium, cut into sticks
- Hummus: 1/2 cup

Instructions:

Preparing Carrots:

- Wash, peel, and cut carrots into sticks.

Serving:

- Dip carrot sticks into hummus before eating.

Benefits:

- Carrots: High in beta-carotene, carrots promote eye health and provide fiber for digestive health.
- Hummus: Made from chickpeas, hummus is a good source of plant-based protein and fiber, aiding in satiety and digestive health.

Rice Cakes with Avocado

Ingredients:

- Rice cakes: 2 cakes
- Avocado: 1/2, sliced or mashed

Instructions:

Preparing Avocado:

- Slice or mash the avocado.

Serving:

- Spread avocado onto rice cakes evenly.

Benefits:

- Rice Cakes: Low in calories and gluten-free, rice cakes offer a crunchy base for snacks.
- Avocado: Rich in healthy fats and potassium, avocados support heart health and provide satiety.

Nuts and Seeds

Ingredients:

- Almonds, walnuts, or pumpkin seeds: A handful

Instructions:

Portioning:

- Grab a handful (around 1 ounce or 28 grams) of your preferred nuts or seeds.

Serving:

- Consume them as they are, or mix them for a variety of flavors and nutrients.

Benefits:

- Nuts and Seeds: Rich in healthy fats, fiber, and antioxidants, they support heart health, aid in weight management, and provide essential nutrients like vitamin E and omega-3 fatty acids.

Cottage Cheese with Pineapple

Ingredients:

- Low-fat cottage cheese: 1/2 cup
- Fresh pineapple: 1/2 cup, diced

Instructions:

Preparation:

- Place the cottage cheese in a bowl.
- Dice fresh pineapple into small pieces.

Serving:

- Mix the diced pineapple with cottage cheese or serve them side by side.

Benefits:

- Cottage Cheese: High in protein and calcium, cottage cheese supports muscle repair and bone health.
- Pineapple: Contains bromelain, an enzyme that aids digestion, and is rich in vitamin C and antioxidants, supporting immune health.

Whole Grain Crackers with Low-Fat Cheese

Ingredients:

- Whole grain crackers: 4-5 pieces
- Low-fat cheese: 1-2 slices or 1/4 cup shredded

Instructions:

Assembly:

- Place the whole grain crackers on a plate.
- Add slices or sprinkle shredded low-fat cheese on the crackers.

Benefits:

- Whole Grain Crackers: Provide fiber and complex carbohydrates, promoting digestive health and offering sustained energy.
- Low-Fat Cheese: A good source of calcium and protein, supporting bone health and muscle repair.

Boiled Edamame

Ingredients:

- Edamame: 1 cup, in pods
- Salt: To taste (optional)

Instructions:

Boiling Edamame:

- Boil a pot of water and add edamame pods.
- Boil for 5-7 minutes until tender.

Seasoning:

- Drain the edamame and season with salt if desired.

Benefits:

- Edamame: High in protein, fiber, and various vitamins and minerals, edamame supports muscle health, aids in weight management, and offers antioxidants.

HOMEMADE TRAIL MIX

Ingredients:

- Assorted nuts: Almonds, cashews, walnuts
- Seeds: Pumpkin seeds, sunflower seeds
- Dried fruits: Raisins, dried cranberries

Instructions:

Mixing Ingredients:

- Combine desired amounts of nuts, seeds, and dried fruits in a bowl.

Portioning:

- Portion out small amounts (around 1/4 cup) into individual servings for snacks.

Benefits:

- Trail Mix: Offers a mix of healthy fats, protein, and a variety of nutrients from nuts, seeds, and dried fruits, providing sustained energy and satiety.

Roasted Chickpeas

Ingredients:

- Canned chickpeas: 1 can (15 oz), drained and rinsed
- Olive oil: 1-2 tablespoons
- Spices: Paprika, garlic powder, cumin (to taste)
- Salt: To taste

Instructions:

Roasting Chickpeas:

- Preheat oven to 400°F (200°C).
- Pat dry the chickpeas and toss with olive oil and spices.
- Spread them on a baking sheet and roast for 25-30 minutes until crispy.

Benefits:

- Chickpeas: High in protein and fiber, chickpeas support digestive health, provide sustained energy, and aid in weight management.

Sliced Cucumbers with Tuna

Ingredients:

- Cucumbers: 1 large, sliced
- Canned tuna: 1 can (5 oz), drained
- Lemon juice: 1 tablespoon
- Salt and pepper: To taste

Instructions:

Preparing Cucumbers:

- Wash and slice the cucumber into rounds or sticks.

Tuna Preparation:

- In a bowl, mix drained tuna with lemon juice, salt, and pepper.

Serving:

- Place a dollop of seasoned tuna on each cucumber slice/stick before consuming.

Benefits:

- Cucumbers: Low in calories and high in water content, cucumbers offer hydration and a good source of vitamins and minerals.
- Tuna: Rich in protein and omega-3 fatty acids, tuna supports muscle repair and heart health.

Low-Fat Popcorn

Ingredients:

- Popcorn kernels: 1/4 cup
- Olive oil: 1-2 teaspoons
- Salt: To taste

Instructions:

Popping Popcorn:

- Use an air popper or stovetop method to pop the kernels.
- Drizzle with olive oil and sprinkle with salt.

Benefits:

- Popcorn: High in fiber and low in calories, popcorn is a whole grain snack that aids in digestion and provides a satisfying crunch.

Bell Pepper Strips with Guacamole

Ingredients:

- Bell peppers: 2 large, sliced into strips
- Avocado: 1 ripe
- Lime juice: Juice of 1 lime
- Salt and pepper: To taste

Instructions:

Preparing Bell Peppers:

- Wash, deseed, and slice the bell peppers into strips.

Guacamole:

- Mash the ripe avocado and mix with lime juice, salt, and pepper.

Serving:

- Use bell pepper strips as dippers for the guacamole.

Benefits:

- Bell Peppers: Rich in vitamin C and antioxidants, bell peppers promote skin health and boost immunity.
- Avocado: Provides healthy fats and is rich in potassium and fiber, supporting heart health and satiety.

Steamed Artichoke

Ingredients:

- Artichoke: 1 medium
- Lemon: 1/2, sliced

- Garlic: 1 clove, crushed (optional)
- Salt: To taste

Instructions:

Preparation:

- Trim the stem of the artichoke and remove any tough outer leaves.

Steaming:

- Place artichoke in a steamer basket with lemon slices and garlic, if using.
- Steam for about 25-35 minutes until tender.

Benefits:

- Artichoke: High in fiber and antioxidants, artichokes support digestive health and may aid in lowering cholesterol levels.

Chia Seed Pudding

Ingredients:

- Chia seeds: 1/4 cup
- Almond milk: 1 cup
- Honey or stevia: To taste
- Vanilla extract: 1 teaspoon (optional)

Instructions:

Mixing:

- In a bowl or jar, mix chia seeds with almond milk and sweetener (honey or stevia) to taste.
- Add vanilla extract for flavor if desired.

Setting:

- Refrigerate for at least 2 hours or overnight until the mixture thickens.

Benefits:

- Chia Seeds: High in fiber, omega-3 fatty acids, and antioxidants, chia seeds support digestive health, provide sustained energy, and may help with weight management.

HARD-BOILED EGGS

Ingredients:

- Eggs: 2-3
- Water: Enough to cover the eggs in a pot

Instructions:

Boiling Eggs:

- Place eggs in a single layer at the bottom of a saucepan or pot.
- Cover with water, ensuring the eggs are fully submerged.
- Bring water to a boil, then immediately remove the pot from the heat, cover, and let the eggs sit for about 9-12 minutes.

Cooling and Peeling:

- Transfer the eggs to an ice bath or run them under cold water until they are cool enough to handle.
- Gently crack the shells and peel off the eggshells.

Benefits:

- Hard-Boiled Eggs: High in protein and essential vitamins like B12, eggs promote muscle repair and provide nutrients for brain health.

Turkey or Chicken Roll-Ups

Ingredients:

- Turkey or chicken deli meat: 4 slices
- Cucumber or lettuce: 4 slices or leaves

Instructions:

Assembly:

- Lay out the turkey or chicken deli slices on a clean surface.
- Place cucumber or lettuce slices on top of each slice.

Rolling:

- Roll up the deli meat with the cucumber or lettuce inside.

Benefits:

- Turkey or Chicken: Provides lean protein and essential nutrients like selenium and phosphorus, supporting muscle health and immune function.
- Cucumber or Lettuce: Low in calories and high in water content, they provide hydration and essential vitamins.

Kale Chips

Ingredients:

- Fresh kale: 1 bunch, washed and dried
- Olive oil: 1-2 tablespoons
- Salt: To taste

Instructions:

Preparation:

- Preheat oven to 300°F (150°C).
- Remove the kale leaves from the stems and tear into bite-sized pieces.

Coating and Baking:

- In a bowl, massage the kale leaves with olive oil and sprinkle with salt.
- Spread the kale pieces on a baking sheet in a single layer.

Baking:

- Bake for 10-15 minutes until the edges are browned and crispy.

Benefits:

- Kale: Packed with vitamins A, K, and C, kale chips offer antioxidants, support bone health, and provide essential nutrients.

Tofu Veggie Skewers

Ingredients:

- Firm tofu: 1 block, cut into cubes
- Assorted veggies: Bell peppers, onions, cherry tomatoes
- Olive oil: 2 tablespoons
- Salt and pepper: To taste

Instructions:

- Assembling Skewers:
- Thread tofu cubes and assorted veggies onto skewers.

Grilling:

- Brush skewers with olive oil and season with salt and pepper.
- Grill for 10-15 minutes, turning occasionally, until tofu and veggies are grilled and slightly charred.

Benefits:

- Tofu: A source of plant-based protein and rich in calcium, tofu supports muscle health and bone strength.
- Assorted Veggies: Offer a range of vitamins, minerals, and antioxidants, supporting overall health and immune function.

Quinoa Salad Cups

Ingredients:

- Cooked quinoa: 2 cups
- Assorted veggies: Cucumbers, cherry tomatoes, bell peppers
- Light vinaigrette: 4 tablespoons
- Lettuce leaves: 8 leaves for cups

Instructions:

Mixing Salad:

- In a bowl, mix cooked quinoa with chopped veggies and light vinaigrette.

Serving:

- Spoon quinoa salad into lettuce cups to serve.

Benefits:

- Quinoa: High in protein and fiber, quinoa supports digestion and provides essential amino acids.
- Assorted Veggies: Offer a variety of nutrients and antioxidants, supporting various bodily functions and overall health.

These snacks offer a variety of nutrients from protein to vitamins and antioxidants, contributing to overall health and satiety. Adjust portions based on individual preferences and dietary needs.

DINNERS

Baked Lemon Herb Chicken

Ingredients:

- Chicken breasts
- Assorted herbs (such as thyme, rosemary, parsley)
- Lemon juice
- Salt and pepper to taste

Instructions:

Preparation:

- Preheat the oven to 375°F (190°C).
- Place the chicken breasts on a baking dish lined with parchment paper or lightly coated with cooking spray.

Seasoning:

- Sprinkle both sides of the chicken breasts with a mix of chopped herbs, salt, and pepper.
- Drizzle lemon juice generously over the chicken.

Baking:

- Bake the chicken in the preheated oven for approximately 25-30 minutes or until the chicken is fully cooked through. Cooking time may vary based on the thickness of the chicken breasts. Ensure the internal temperature reaches 165°F (74°C).

Grilled Fish Tacos

Ingredients:

- Fish fillets (such as cod or tilapia)
- Soft corn tortillas
- Cabbage slaw (shredded cabbage, carrots, tossed with a light vinaigrette)
- Salsa

Instructions:

Grilling the Fish:

- Preheat your grill to medium-high heat.
- Season the fish fillets with a sprinkle of salt, pepper, and a touch of olive oil.
- Grill the fish for about 3-4 minutes per side until they are cooked through and easily flake with a fork.

Preparing Tortillas:

- Warm the corn tortillas on the grill for a minute or so on each side until they're soft and pliable.

Assembling Tacos:

- Place a portion of grilled fish on each tortilla.
- Top it with cabbage slaw and salsa.

QUINOA-STUFFED PEPPERS

Ingredients:

- Bell peppers (any color)
- Quinoa
- Black beans (canned or cooked)
- Chopped vegetables (such as onions, corn, diced tomatoes)
- Spices (cumin, paprika, garlic powder)
- Low-sodium vegetable or chicken broth

Instructions:

Preparation:

- Preheat the oven to 375°F (190°C).

Preparing Peppers:

- Cut the tops off the bell peppers and remove the seeds and membranes.

Making Filling:

- Cook quinoa as per package instructions.
- Sauté chopped vegetables until softened. Add cooked quinoa, black beans, and spices. Mix well and add a bit of broth to moisten the mixture.

Stuffing Peppers:

- Spoon the quinoa and vegetable mixture into each pepper until generously filled.

Baking:

- Place the stuffed peppers in a baking dish and bake for about 25-30 minutes until the peppers are tender and the filling is heated through.

Turkey Meatballs with Zucchini Noodles

Ingredients:

- For Turkey Meatballs:
- 1 pound ground turkey
- Salt and pepper to taste
- Preferred spices (such as garlic powder, onion powder, Italian seasoning)
- For Zucchini Noodles:
- 2-3 medium-sized zucchinis (spiralized or thinly sliced)
- Olive oil
- Salt and pepper to taste
- For Serving:
- Marinara sauce (homemade or store-bought)
- Fresh herbs (optional, for garnish)

Instructions:

Preparing Turkey Meatballs:
- Preheat the oven to 375°F (190°C).
- In a mixing bowl, combine the ground turkey with salt, pepper, and preferred spices.
- Shape the seasoned turkey into meatballs and place them on a baking sheet lined with parchment paper.
- Bake for 15-20 minutes until the meatballs are cooked through.

Cooking Zucchini Noodles:
- Heat olive oil in a skillet over medium heat.
- Add the zucchini noodles and sauté for 3-5 minutes until they are slightly softened but still have a bit of crunch. Season with salt and pepper.

Assembly:
- Serve the cooked turkey meatballs over the sautéed zucchini noodles.
- Pour marinara sauce over the meatballs and noodles.
- Garnish with fresh herbs if desired.

Baked Salmon with Steamed Vegetables

Ingredients:

For Salmon:

- Salmon fillets (4-6 ounces each)
- Salt, pepper, and preferred seasoning (like lemon pepper or dill)

For Steamed Vegetables:

- 2 cups broccoli florets
- 1 cup sliced carrots
- 2 cups cauliflower florets
- Olive oil
- Salt and pepper to taste

For Serving:

- Lemon wedges (optional, for garnish)

Instructions:

Preparing Salmon:

- Preheat the oven to 400°F (200°C).
- Season the salmon fillets with salt, pepper, and preferred seasoning. Drizzle with olive oil.
- Place the seasoned salmon fillets on a baking sheet lined with parchment paper.
- Bake for 12-15 minutes until the salmon is cooked through and flakes easily with a fork.

Steaming Vegetables:

- Steam broccoli, carrots, and cauliflower until they are tender-crisp. You can use a steamer basket or a microwave-safe dish with a bit of water.

Assembly:

- Serve the baked salmon fillets alongside the steamed vegetables.
- Garnish with lemon wedges if desired.

Veggie Stir-Fry with Tofu

Ingredients:

For Stir-Fry:

- 1 block firm tofu, drained and cubed
- Assorted vegetables (bell peppers, broccoli, snap peas, carrots, etc.)
- Olive oil
- Low-sodium soy sauce or stir-fry sauce

For Serving:

- Cooked brown rice

Instructions:

Preparing Tofu and Vegetables:

- Heat olive oil in a large skillet or wok over medium-high heat.
- Add cubed tofu and stir-fry until golden brown. Remove tofu from the pan and set aside.
- In the same pan, stir-fry assorted vegetables until tender-crisp.

Combining Tofu and Vegetables:

- Add the cooked tofu back into the pan with the vegetables.
- Pour low-sodium soy sauce or stir-fry sauce over tofu and vegetables. Toss to combine and heat through.

Serving:

- Serve the veggie stir-fry over cooked brown rice.

Lemon Garlic Shrimp Skewers

Ingredients:

For Shrimp Skewers:

- 1 pound large shrimp, peeled and deveined
- 1/4 cup fresh lemon juice
- 3 cloves garlic, minced
- 2 tablespoons chopped fresh herbs (parsley, thyme, rosemary)
- 2 tablespoons olive oil
- Salt and pepper to taste

Instructions:

Marinating Shrimp:

- In a mixing bowl, combine the shrimp with lemon juice, minced garlic, chopped herbs, olive oil, salt, and pepper. Mix well to coat the shrimp evenly and let it marinate for 15-20 minutes.

Cooking Shrimp:

- Preheat the grill or oven.
- Thread the marinated shrimp onto skewers.
- Grill or bake the shrimp skewers for 2-3 minutes per side until they turn pink and are cooked through.

Baked Sweet Potato with Grilled Chicken

Ingredients:

For Sweet Potatoes:

- 4 medium sweet potatoes
- Olive oil

- Salt and pepper to taste

For Grilled Chicken:

- 4 chicken breasts
- Preferred seasoning (garlic powder, paprika, Italian seasoning)

Instructions:

Preparing Sweet Potatoes:

- Preheat the oven to 400°F (200°C).
- Wash and dry the sweet potatoes. Pierce them several times with a fork.
- Rub olive oil, salt, and pepper onto the sweet potatoes. Place them on a baking sheet.
- Bake for 45-60 minutes until tender.

Grilling Chicken:

- Season chicken breasts with preferred spices.
- Grill the chicken over medium-high heat until cooked through, about 5-7 minutes per side.

Assembly:

- Cut open the baked sweet potatoes.
- Top them with grilled chicken breasts.

Lentil Soup

Ingredients:

For Lentil Soup:

- 1 cup dry lentils
- 2 carrots, chopped

- 2 stalks celery, chopped
- 6 cups low-sodium vegetable or chicken broth
- 2 tablespoons olive oil
- Herbs and spices (bay leaves, thyme, cumin)
- Salt and pepper to taste

Instructions:

Cooking Lentil Soup:

- In a pot, heat olive oil over medium heat.
- Sauté chopped carrots and celery until slightly softened.
- Add dry lentils, broth, herbs, salt, and pepper. Bring to a boil, then simmer for 25-30 minutes until lentils are tender.

SPINACH AND MUSHROOM OMELETTE

Ingredients:

For Omelette:

- 4 eggs
- 1 cup fresh spinach, chopped
- 1 cup sliced mushrooms
- 1/2 cup low-fat cheese (optional)
- Olive oil or cooking spray
- Salt and pepper to taste

Instructions:

Making Omelette:

- Heat olive oil or cooking spray in a non-stick skillet over medium heat.
- Sauté chopped spinach and sliced mushrooms until spinach wilts and mushrooms are cooked.
- In a bowl, beat eggs with salt and pepper.
- Pour the beaten eggs into the skillet over the cooked vegetables.

- Cook until the eggs are set but still slightly moist on top.
- Sprinkle low-fat cheese over the omelette if desired.
- Fold the omelette in half and serve.

Baked Cod with Herbs

Ingredients:

- Cod fillets: 4 pieces
- Assorted herbs: 2 tablespoons each of parsley, dill, and thyme (or herbs of choice)
- Olive oil: 2 tablespoons
- Salt and pepper: To taste

Instructions:

Preparation:

- Preheat the oven to 375°F (190°C).
- Pat dry the cod fillets using paper towels.

Seasoning:

- Drizzle a little olive oil over the cod fillets, spreading it evenly.
- Season both sides of the cod fillets with salt, pepper, and the assortment of herbs.

Baking:

- Place the seasoned cod fillets on a baking sheet lined with parchment paper or lightly greased.
- Bake in the preheated oven for about 12-15 minutes or until the fish is flaky and easily separates with a fork.

Turkey and Vegetable Stir-Fry

Ingredients:

- Sliced turkey breast: 1 pound
- Bell peppers: 2, sliced
- Snap peas: 1 cup
- Onions: 1 large, sliced
- Low-sodium soy sauce or stir-fry sauce: 3 tablespoons
- Olive oil: 2 tablespoons
- Cooked brown rice: 2 cups (optional, for serving)

Instructions:

Stir-Frying:

- Heat olive oil in a large skillet or wok over medium-high heat.
- Add sliced turkey breast and stir-fry until it's lightly browned and cooked through.

Adding Vegetables:

- Add sliced bell peppers, snap peas, and onions to the skillet.
- Stir-fry everything together for a few minutes until the vegetables are tender-crisp.

Sauce and Serving:

- Pour low-sodium soy sauce or stir-fry sauce over the turkey and vegetables.
- Serve the turkey and vegetable stir-fry over cooked brown rice if desired.

Quinoa and Black Bean Bowl

Ingredients:

- Cooked quinoa: 2 cups
- Black beans: 1 can (15 oz), drained and rinsed
- Corn kernels: 1 cup
- Diced tomatoes: 1 cup
- Lime juice: Juice of 1 lime
- Salt and pepper: To taste
- Fresh cilantro for garnish: Optional

Instructions:

Mixing Ingredients:

- In a bowl, combine cooked quinoa, black beans, corn kernels, and diced tomatoes.

Seasoning:

- Squeeze fresh lime juice over the mixture.
- Add salt and pepper to taste.

Garnish and Serve:

- Garnish with fresh cilantro if desired.
- Serve the quinoa and black bean bowl as a wholesome dish on its own or as a side.

Grilled Chicken Salad

Ingredients:

- Grilled chicken strips: 2 cups
- Mixed greens: 6 cups (lettuce, spinach, arugula, etc.)
- Cucumbers: 1 large, sliced
- Tomatoes: 2 medium, sliced
- Light vinaigrette dressing: 4 tablespoons

Instructions:

Preparing Salad:

- In a large salad bowl, toss together mixed greens, sliced cucumbers, and tomatoes.

Adding Chicken:

- Place grilled chicken strips on top of the mixed greens.

Dressing:

- Drizzle the light vinaigrette dressing over the salad just before serving or serve it on the side.

Baked Tofu with Roasted Vegetables

Ingredients:

- Tofu: 1 block, pressed and sliced
- Assorted vegetables: Your choice (such as bell peppers, zucchini, carrots)
- Spice rub: Your preferred seasoning mix
- Olive oil: 2 tablespoons
- Salt and pepper: To taste

Instructions:

Preparation:

- Preheat the oven to 375°F (190°C).
- Press the tofu to remove excess water and slice it into desired shapes.
- Cut assorted vegetables into bite-sized pieces.

Seasoning:

- Rub the tofu slices with the spice rub evenly on both sides.
- Toss the assorted vegetables with olive oil, salt, and pepper.

Baking:

- Place the seasoned tofu on one baking sheet and the seasoned vegetables on another.
- Bake in the preheated oven for about 20-25 minutes or until the tofu is golden and the vegetables are tender, flipping halfway through.

Eggplant Rollatini

Ingredients:

- Eggplant: 2 large, thinly sliced lengthwise
- Low-fat ricotta cheese: 1 cup
- Spinach: 1 cup, cooked and drained
- Marinara sauce: 2 cups
- Mozzarella cheese: 1 cup, shredded (optional)
- Olive oil: 2 tablespoons
- Salt and pepper: To taste

Instructions:

Preparation:

- Preheat the oven to 375°F (190°C).

- Lay out eggplant slices and sprinkle with salt. Let sit for 10 minutes, then pat dry with paper towels.

Filling:

- In a bowl, mix together low-fat ricotta cheese, cooked spinach, salt, and pepper.

Assembly:

- Spread a spoonful of the ricotta mixture onto each eggplant slice and roll them up.

Baking:

- Pour marinara sauce into a baking dish.
- Place the eggplant rolls in the dish, seam side down.
- Optionally, sprinkle shredded mozzarella cheese on top.
- Bake for about 25-30 minutes until the cheese is bubbly and golden.

Turkey Chili

Ingredients:

- Lean ground turkey: 1 pound
- Kidney beans: 1 can (15 oz), drained and rinsed
- Tomatoes: 1 can (14 oz), diced
- Chili spices: 2 tablespoons chili powder, 1 teaspoon cumin, 1 teaspoon paprika
- Olive oil: 2 tablespoons
- Onion: 1 medium, chopped
- Garlic: 2 cloves, minced
- Salt and pepper: To taste

Instructions:

Cooking Turkey:

- Heat olive oil in a large pot over medium heat.
- Add chopped onions and minced garlic, sauté until softened.
- Add ground turkey, cook until browned, breaking it up with a spoon as it cooks.

Adding Ingredients:
- Stir in kidney beans, diced tomatoes, and chili spices.
- Season with salt and pepper to taste.

Simmering:
- Reduce heat to low, cover, and simmer for 30-40 minutes, stirring occasionally.

Baked Cod with Mango Salsa

Ingredients:

- Cod fillets: 4 pieces
- Mango: 1 ripe, diced
- Red onion: 1/2 small, finely chopped
- Fresh cilantro: 1/4 cup, chopped
- Lime juice: Juice of 1 lime
- Jalapeño: 1 small, seeded and finely chopped (optional)
- Salt and pepper: To taste

Instructions:

Baking Cod:
- Preheat the oven to 375°F (190°C).
- Place the cod fillets on a baking sheet lined with parchment paper.
- Season with salt and pepper, then bake for 12-15 minutes or until cooked through.

Making Mango Salsa:
- In a bowl, mix diced mango, chopped red onion, cilantro, lime juice, and jalapeño if using.
- Season with salt and pepper to taste.

Serving:
- Top the baked cod with the prepared mango salsa before serving.

Vegetable Curry with Brown Rice

Ingredients:

- Assorted vegetables: Carrots, bell peppers, cauliflower, peas, etc. (about 4 cups, chopped)
- Curry sauce: 2 cups prepared or use curry paste with coconut milk
- Brown rice: 2 cups, cooked
- Olive oil: 2 tablespoons
- Onion: 1 medium, chopped
- Garlic: 2 cloves, minced
- Salt: To taste

Instructions:

Sautéing Vegetables:
- Heat olive oil in a pan over medium heat.
- Add chopped onions and minced garlic, sauté until fragrant.
- Add assorted vegetables and sauté for 5-7 minutes until slightly tender.

Adding Sauce and Simmering:
- Pour curry sauce over the vegetables, stirring to coat.
- Simmer for 10-15 minutes until the vegetables are cooked through.

Serving:
- Serve the vegetable curry over cooked brown rice.

Chicken and Vegetable Skewers

Ingredients:
- Chicken breasts: 2, cut into chunks
- Assorted vegetables: Bell peppers, onions, cherry tomatoes, etc.
- Olive oil: 2 tablespoons
- Salt and pepper: To taste
- Skewers: Wooden or metal skewers

Instructions:

Preparation:
- Preheat grill to medium-high heat.
- Thread chicken chunks and assorted vegetables onto skewers.

Grilling:
- Brush skewers with olive oil and season with salt and pepper.
- Grill skewers for 10-15 minutes, turning occasionally until chicken is cooked and vegetables are tender.

Serving:
- Serve the chicken and vegetable skewers with a side salad.

CONCLUSION

In concluding this comprehensive guide, I extend my heartfelt gratitude to every reader who embarked on this journey toward gallbladder health and a fulfilling lifestyle. Together, we've navigated the intricate landscape of living without a gallbladder or striving to maintain its well-being.

My fervent hope is that this book has been more than just a guide; it's my aspiration that it has been a catalyst for positive change. For some, it may have provided solace, offering reassurance in making vital decisions about gallbladder health. To others, perhaps, it has alleviated the fear of living without this organ and shown that life can indeed be vibrant without it.

As an author deeply invested in the well-being of my readers, I sincerely hope that the insights shared within these pages have transformed lives for the better. Whether it's adopting healthier dietary habits, finding ways to manage pain, or embracing life after gallbladder removal, my aim was to empower and inspire.

Your decision to explore this guide demonstrates your commitment to your well-being, and for that, I am immensely grateful. I encourage you to embrace these newfound insights, integrate them into your daily life, and witness the positive changes they bring.

Wishing each of you continued success on your journey toward optimal health and well-being. May this book serve as a constant companion, offering guidance and support whenever needed.

Lastly, if this book has made a positive impact on your life, I kindly invite you to share your experiences and leave a review on Amazon. Your feedback is invaluable, not only for me as an author but also for others seeking guidance on their path to gallbladder health.

Thank you for allowing me to be a part of your journey.

Warm regards

EXPLORE MORE GREAT READS

The PCOS Diet Cookbook:
Strategies and Recipes for Overcoming PCOS Symptoms, Maximizing Fertility, and Improving Overall Health

ASIN: B0CTKXBVZ9
ASIN: B0CTHTZV45

The Anti-Inflammatory Diet:
Your Guide to Reducing Inflammation and Improving Your Health

ASIN: B0CNKRZB56
ASIN: B0CNKKC8MT
ASIN: B0CV2TWM5N

Somatic Psychotherapy Handbook:
Illuminating the Depths of Body-Centered TherapyA Comprehensive Guide

ASIN: B0CZ155HS2
ASIN: B0CYVL3228

Healthy Diabetic Smoothies Cookbook for Beginners:
70 Diabetic-Friendly Colorful Recipe Photos with Glycemic Index (GL), Calorie, and Nutritional Information

ASIN: B0CS3N9C6K
ASIN: B0CR9GMVXT

Healthy Quick & Easy Vegetable Smoothie Recipe Book:
Green Blends for Beginners - Simple, Delicious, Plant-Based Drinks with Up to 5 Ingredients for Weight Loss

ASIN: B0CS9P4GN5
ASIN: B0CSZF3P4Z

Kids Smoothie Recipe Book:
A-Z Guide to Healthy, Yummy, Nutritious Blends They'll Love Making. Illustrated for Kids

ASIN: B0D2JC8J4H
ASIN: B0D2391MWV

The Ultimate Coffee Recipe Book: Unlock 180 Creative Coffee Delights for Enthusiasts

ASIN: B0CVVJ6Q8B
ASIN: B0CVXSQL15
ASIN: B0CVSQTG8B

Healthy Smoothie Recipe Book for Weight Loss: 65 Blender Recipes Under 300 Calories for Good Health

ASIN: B0CZ11DR3H
ASIN: B0CYQM3T3L

Printed in Great Britain
by Amazon

46274628R00066